# Strategies and Lessons
## for Improving
# Basic Early
# Literacy Skills

*To the millions of children who after one, two, three, or four years in school still are not reading proficiently . . . we share your pain and hope for a better future.*

# Strategies and Lessons for Improving
# Basic Early Literacy Skills

Bob Algozzine • Mary Beth Marr
Tina McClanahan • Emme Barnes

Skyhorse Publishing

Visit our website at www.skyhorsepublishing.com.

10 9 8 7 6 5 4 3 2 1

Library of Congress Cataloging-in-Publication Data is available on file.

ISBN: 978-1-61608-584-1

Printed in Canada

# Table of Contents

# Acknowledgments

Collectively we are grateful to administrators, teachers, and children in Charlotte-Mecklenburg schools, especially Idlewild Elementary, Montclaire Elementary, Piney Grove Elementary, and Winterfield Elementary, for continuing support of our efforts to identify, practice, and assess effective early literacy instruction and for providing outstanding evidence that good teaching works. We are also thankful for the interest and support of Kathleen McLane and our Corwin team in preparing this book. Individually, we acknowledge others below:

Bob Algozzine is grateful for the opportunity to have worked with Beth, Tina, and Emme on this book and thankful for the great professionalism, friendship, and teaching they shared while doing it and other collaborative projects. He is also thankful for his family who daily remind him of the wonders, benefits, and enduring joys of fatherhood.

Mary Beth Marr thanks Bob for his wisdom and ability to see promise and possibilities in today's challenging classrooms. She thanks Tina and Emme for their commitment to this project and instructional expertise essential to the development of these lessons. Finally, she thanks her family for their love and support.

Tina McClanahan is blessed beyond measure both professionally and personally. She is thankful for the opportunity to have collaborated with Bob, Beth, and Emme and for the patience and support of her family as she worked on this project.

Emme Barnes is thankful for the opportunity to have worked with Bob, Beth, and Tina on this book. Their commitment to early literacy instruction for all children is a model for others to follow. She is also grateful to her parents and husband for their love, support, and guidance. She sends special thanks to her wonderful children Emma Grace and Mac, who are her constant "sunshines."

Corwin Press would like to extend additional thanks to the following for their contributions to the book:

Jessie Fries-Kraemer
Teacher, Fifth Grade and Literacy
Eubank Elementary School
Albuquerque, New Mexico

Jill Denson
First Grade, Literacy
Bryan Elementary School
Omaha, Nebraska

Meg L. Miller
Literacy Specialist
Martin Luther King Jr. Elementary School
Urbana, Illinois

Tanya Phaturos
Reading Specialist
Park Elementary School
Holbrook, Arizona

Wanda Mangum
K–12 Language Arts Instructional Coach
Gwinnett County Public School
Gwinnett, Georgia

# About the Authors

**Bob Algozzine**, PhD, is professor in the Department of Educational Leadership at the University of North Carolina and co-project director of the U.S. Department of Education–supported Behavior and Reading Improvement Center. With 25 years of research experience and extensive firsthand knowledge of teaching students classified as seriously emotionally disturbed (and other equally useless terms), Algozzine is a uniquely qualified staff developer, conference speaker, and teacher of behavior management and effective teaching courses.

As an active partner and collaborator with professionals in the Charlotte-Mecklenburg schools in North Carolina and as an editor of several journals focused on special education, Algozzine keeps his finger on the pulse of current special education practice. He has written more than 250 manuscripts on special education topics, authoring many popular books and textbooks on how to manage emotional and social behavior problems. Through *Strategies and Lessons for Improving Basic Early Literacy Skills*, Algozzine hopes to continue to help improve the lives of students with special needs—and the professionals who teach them.

**Mary Beth Marr** is an Associate Professor in Education at Meredith College in Raleigh, North Carolina. She teaches graduate and undergraduate courses in literacy education. The *Strategies and Lessons for Improving Basic Early Literacy Skills* text was completed during her appointment as a Research Associate with the Behavior and Reading Improvement Center at UNC Charlotte. Dr. Marr's research interests focus on early literacy and struggling readers.

**Tina McClanahan** has worked for the Charlotte-Mecklenburg School (CMS) system since her graduation from West Virginia State College. During her time with CMS, she has held the positions of classroom teacher, literacy teacher, Reading Recovery teacher, and K–2 Literacy Facilitator, and is currently a Pre–K Literacy Facilitator. She also worked for the Behavior and Reading Improvement

Center, University of North Carolina at Charlotte, as a Center Support Coordinating teacher and received National Board status in 2001 as an Early Childhood Generalist (ECGEN). She resides in Matthews, North Carolina, with her husband and two daughters.

 **Emme Barnes** is currently a literacy facilitator in the Charlotte-Mecklenburg School system working with teachers, students, and parents to develop literacy skills in elementary-age students. She has taught first and second grade classes in Title One, large suburban schools, and at The American School of Madrid. Her formal education includes a BS in Elementary Education from the University of North Carolina at Greensboro and a Master of Education degree in Reading, Language, and Literacy from The University of North Carolina at Charlotte. She is on the Advisory Board for Reach Out and Read Charlotte and is a past recipient of the Ten Outstanding Young Charlotteans Award given by the Charlotte Jaycees for her work with literacy in the community.

# 1

# Introduction

*While there are no easy answers or quick solutions for optimizing reading achievement, an extensive knowledge base now exists to show us the skills children must learn in order to read well. These skills provide the basis for sound curriculum decisions and instructional approaches that can help prevent the predictable consequences of early reading failure.*

National Institute for Literacy (2003)

*Strategies and Lessons for Improving Basic Early Literacy Skills* is a collection of practical activities and building blocks for helping children learn to read. The materials in this book are resources designed by teachers to build proficiency in key areas of beginning reading: recognizing and naming letters; hearing and manipulating sounds in words; associating sounds with letters and using them to form words; and reading words in connected text effortlessly, automatically, and accurately. We grouped and identified each activity by the early literacy skill and the area of instruction it addresses as well as by a *Dynamic Indicators of Basic Early Literacy Skills* (DIBELS) benchmark indicator used to assess it. We present a purpose for each activity, including an exemplary Standard Course of Study (SCOS) Competency Goal Objective, grouping strategies, instructional strategies, and differentiation ideas. Handouts, presentation masters, and related readings are also part of this resource.

We wrote the book for elementary school teachers who use DIBELS or similarly focused early literacy skills assessments to measure student progress. We have included practical suggestions for activities and lessons in a format that is easy to use to help children improve their early literacy skills. We also present case studies illustrating use in real classrooms. We have used this content effectively to help teachers use assessment information to inform their instruction.

Literacy skills are the foundation for achievement of a fundamental goal of education: all children reading by the end of third grade. Regular assessment of progress toward benchmarks on key indicators provides the foundation for teaching critical literacy skills. *Strategies and Lessons for Improving Basic Early Literacy Skills Activities* links outcomes of selected early literacy skills assessments to instruction.

# ORGANIZATIONAL FRAMEWORK

Each set of activities addresses a different early literacy skill and different benchmarks on the *Dynamic Indicators of Basic Early Literacy Skills* (DIBELS) assessments. We illustrate the scope and content of the activities below:

**Table 1.1**  Basic Early Literacy Skills (BELS) Scope and Content

| Early Literacy Skill | Dynamic Indicators of Basic Early Literacy Skills | Basic Early Literacy Skills Activities |
|---|---|---|
| Ability to recognize and name letters | Letter Naming Fluency | • Distinguishing Letters from Non-Letters<br>• Distinguishing Letter Forms<br>  ○ Tall Letters<br>  ○ Short Circular Letters<br>  ○ Short Stick Letters<br>  ○ Short Hump Letters<br>  ○ Hanging Letters<br>• Distinguishing Same and Different Letters<br>• Distinguishing Uppercase and Lowercase Letters<br>  ○ Differentiating Using American Sign Language<br>  ○ Differentiating Using Sense of Touch<br>• Distinguishing Letter/Sound (Using Sense of Touch) |
| Ability to hear and manipulate sounds in words | Initial Sound Fluency | • Silly Sentence—Part 1<br>• Picture/Sound Charts<br>• Letter/Sound Books—Part 1<br>• Letter/Sound Books—Part 2<br>• Sound Collages<br>• Sound Identification Game<br>• Picture/Sound Identification Game |
|  | Phoneme Segmentation Fluency | • "Stretching" Sounds in Words<br>• Elkonin Boxes—Identifying Sounds With Fingers<br>• Elkonin Boxes— Pushing Sounds |

| Early Literacy Skill | Dynamic Indicators of Basic Early Literacy Skills | Basic Early Literacy Skills Activities |
|---|---|---|
| | | • Elkonin Boxes—Sound Boxes<br>• Elkonin Boxes—Transition Boxes<br>• Elkonin Boxes—Letter Boxes |
| Ability to associate sounds with letters and use them to form words | Nonsense Word Fluency | • Distinguishing Letters/Sounds Using Sense of Touch<br>• Sound/Letter BINGO<br>• Letter/Sound BINGO<br>• Sound Identification Game<br>• Making and Breaking Using Magnetic Letters<br>• Blending (VC)<br>• Blending (CVC)<br>• Sorting Beginning Consonant Sounds<br>• Sound Line<br>• Word Wheel<br>• Flip Books<br>• Slide-a-Word<br>• Word Scramble<br>• Word Maker<br>• Roll the Dice<br>• MATCH!<br>• RINGO!<br>• Go Fish |
| Ability to read words in connected text effortlessly, automatically, and fluently | Oral Reading Fluency | • Reading Punctuation<br>• Reading Punctuation: Period, Exclamation Point, Question Mark<br>• Reading Text in Phrases to Promote Fluency<br>• Reading Fine and Bold Printed Text as Author Intended<br>• Reading Dialogue |

## USING ASSESSMENT TO INFORM INSTRUCTION

Effective teaching uses information from ongoing assessments to inform instruction. This means that effective teachers informally and formally assess their students' current levels of skill development and analyze the performance to identify what to teach. They also use the information to decide on the type of instruction needed by individual students. When a student is performing as expected compared to his neighbors and peers, effective teachers provide continuing instruction grounded in principles and practices that have been effective with the student in the past. When a student is not performing as expected compared to his neighbors and peers, effective teachers adjust their teaching to support individual learning needs and foster success. Assessment data, especially standardized, state testing outcomes, rarely provide the kind of specific information that classroom teachers need for instruction. Assessments that are productive in this regard are conducted a minimum of three times a year or on a routine basis (i.e., weekly, monthly, or quarterly) using comparable and multiple test forms to (a) estimate rates of reading improvement, (b) identify children who are not demonstrating adequate progress and therefore require additional or different forms of instruction, and/or (c) compare the efficacy of different forms of instruction for struggling learners so that more effective, individualized instructional programs can be put in place for them.

The *Dynamic Indicators of Basic Early Literacy Skills* (DIBELS) is a set of standardized, individually administered measures of early literacy development (http://dibels.uoregon.edu/). They are short (one minute) proficiency measures used to regularly monitor the development of pre-reading and early reading skills. Results can be used to evaluate individual student development as well as to provide direction and feedback to inform instruction. Decision rules or benchmarks provided by the developers of DIBELS for use in preparing instructional recommendations for children in kindergarten and first grade are in the following tables.

*Strategies and Lessons for Improving Basic Early Literacy Skills Activities* is a set of teacher-developed, evidence-based instructional materials for improving the performance and skills of children needing strategic and intensive instruction. They are brief, multilevel activities grounded in principles and practices of effective assessment and instruction. To be most effective, instruction must be grounded in accurate assessment information. Our lessons bridge the gap between early literacy assessments and the expectations and content of core reading programs. As illustrated in Table 1.3, when problems arise, problem solving grounded in different types of assessments leads to solutions.

# INCORPORATING BASIC EARLY LITERACY SKILLS (BELS) INTO THE LITERACY BLOCK

Many teachers use DIBELS or similar early literacy assessment data to place students in instructional groups and then provide targeted instruction to meet the students' needs. There are several models for this instruction. We summarize three typical models below to help teachers plan and implement the BELS activities into their existing literacy instructional period.

### Whole Class Instruction/Independent Work Time

In this instructional model, daily whole class reading instruction is followed by independent work time (IWT). Reading instruction occurs using a commercial reading series (Houghton Mifflin, Open Court, etc.) for roughly a 45–60 minute time period. IWT then follows for approximately 30 minutes. During this time, children work independently and the teacher may select students for

**Table 1.2** DIBELS Benchmark Goals and Indicators of Risk

Kindergarten

| | DIBELS Kindergarten Benchmark Goals and Indicators of Risk | | | | | |
| | Three Assessment Periods Per Year | | | | | |
| | Benchmark Assessment | | | | | |
| Indicator | Beginning of Year Month 1–3 | | Middle of Year Month 4–6 | | End of Year Month 7–10 | |
| | Scores | Status | Scores | Status | Scores | Status |
| Initial Sound Fluency | ISF < 4 | At risk | ISF < 10 | Deficit | | |
| | 4 <= ISF < 8 | Some risk | 10 <= ISF < 25 | Emerging | | |
| | ISF >= 8 | Low risk | ISF >= 25 | Established | | |
| Letter Naming Fluency | LNF < 2 | At risk | LNF < 15 | At risk | LNF < 29 | At risk |
| | 2 <= LNF < 8 | Some risk | 15 <= LNF < 27 | Some risk | 29 <= LNF < 40 | Some risk |
| | LNF >= 8 | Low risk | LNF >= 27 | Low risk | LNF >= 40 | Low risk |
| Phoneme Segmentation Fluency | | | PSF < 7 | At risk | PSF < 10 | Deficit |
| | | | 7 <= PSF < 18 | Some risk | 10 <= PSF < 35 | Emerging |
| | | | PSF >= 18 | Low risk | PSF >= 35 | Established |
| Nonsense Word Fluency | | | NWF < 5 | At risk | NWF < 15 | At risk |
| | | | 5 <= NWF < 13 | Some risk | 15 <= NWF < 25 | Some risk |
| | | | NWF >= 13 | Low risk | NWF >= 25 | Low risk |

SOURCE: © University of Oregon Center on Teaching and Learning, http://dibels.uoregon.edu/benchmark.php

*(Continued)*

**Table 1.2** (Continued)

First Grade

| Indicator | DIBELS First Grade Benchmark Goals and Indicators of Risk | | | | | |
| --- | --- | --- | --- | --- | --- | --- |
| | Three Assessment Periods Per Year | | | | | |
| | Benchmark Assessment | | | | | |
| | Beginning of Year Month 1–3 | | Middle of Year Month 4–6 | | End of Year Month 7–10 | |
| | Scores | Status | Scores | Status | Scores | Status |
| Letter Naming Fluency | LNF < 25 | At risk | | | | |
| | 25 <= LNF < 37 | Some risk | | | | |
| | LNF >= 37 | Low risk | | | | |
| Phoneme Segmentation Fluency | PSF < 10 | Deficit | PSF < 10 | Deficit | PSF < 10 | Deficit |
| | 10 <= PSF < 35 | Emerging | 10 <= PSF < 35 | Emerging | 10 <= PSF < 35 | Emerging |
| | PSF >= 35 | Established | PSF >= 35 | Established | PSF >= 35 | Established |
| Nonsense Word Fluency | NWF < 13 | At risk | NWF < 30 | Deficit | NWF < 30 | Deficit |
| | 13 <= NWF < 24 | Some risk | 30 <= NWF < 50 | Emerging | 30 <= NWF < 50 | Emerging |
| | NWF >= 24 | Low risk | NWF >= 50 | Established | NWF >= 50 | Established |
| Oral Reading | | | ORF < 8 | At risk | ORF < 20 | At risk |
| | | | 8 <= ORF < 20 | Some risk | 20 <= ORF < 40 | Some risk |
| | | | ORF >= 20 | Low risk | ORF >= 40 | Low risk |

SOURCE: © University of Oregon Center on Teaching and Learning, http://dibels.uoregon.edu/benchmark.php

**Table 1.3**   Assessment Drives Instruction

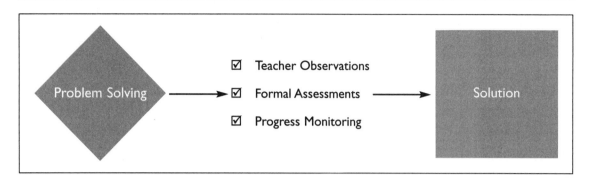

**Table 1.4**   Reading Instructional Models

| Whole Class/IWT (1½–2 hours) | Whole Class/Block (1 hour—reading ) | Whole Class/Four Blocks (2 hours) |
|---|---|---|
| *Whole Class Instruction* (45–60 minutes) | *Guided Reading Groups* 4 groups, 15 minutes each | *Guided Reading* (30 minutes) |
| *IWT* 30 minutes (2 groups, 15 minutes each, teacher directed) BELS lessons | *Small Skills Groups* (Teacher Assistant) BELS lessons | *Writing* (30 minutes) |
| *Literacy Centers* (Independent) BELS activities | *Literacy Centers* (Independent) BELS activities | *Word Work* (30 minutes) BELS lessons/activities (whole class or small group) *Independent Reading* (30 minutes) |

skills groups based on assessment information. Teaching during this time typically involves preteaching, reteaching, or reinforcement. Teachers can easily follow the 10–12 minute BELS lessons to address student needs in phonemic awareness, alphabetic knowledge, phonics, and fluency. We suggest meeting with only two skills groups during the 30-minute block. The two lower skills groups (e.g., initial sound fluency, phoneme segmentation) may meet with the teacher three out of the five days, while the medium and high groups (nonsense word, reading fluency) meet with the teacher two out of the five days. Depending upon the skill level and independent work habits of the students, many of these activities can be completed as independent literacy centers (e.g., letter/sound books, sorting consonant sounds, Slide-a-Word).

### Guided Reading/Literacy Center/Skill Group Instruction

Reading instruction in this model occurs within a 60-minute block of time. The teacher meets with small groups of students (4–6) to direct guided reading groups using leveled books. Each group meets for roughly 15 minutes, while the other students in the classroom are working independently and completing literacy centers. A teacher assistant may also work one on one or with small groups of students during this time. The BELS lessons, with an explicit lesson structure, become an excellent resource for the teacher assistant during the small-group lessons. In addition, students can complete BELS activities independently or at a literacy center to reinforce their literacy skills.

### Whole Class Instruction/Four Blocks Reading Model

This instructional model is referred to as the Four Blocks framework (Cunningham, Hall, & Defee, 1991, 1998; Cunningham, Hall, & Sigmon, 1999). Literacy instruction is divided into four 30-minute periods. Within this structure, 30 minutes are allocated for guided reading instruction, 30 minutes for writing instruction, 30 minutes for independent reading, and 30 minutes for "word work" or word analysis skills. These four instructional periods typically are taught with the whole class. The BELS lessons can easily be adapted for the whole class during the word work phase of the literacy period. If needed, the teacher or assistant could also select targeted students to reteach or practice needed skills using the BELS activities during this time.

We feel that the BELS activities are unique. The lessons are easy to follow and *written explicitly* to provide modeling, guided instructional practice, and independent practice; each also has a "product" associated with it for use in evaluating progress and providing accountability markers. This clear structure gives the necessary support for new teachers or teaching assistants as they become familiar with early literacy skills and strategies. When students can work independently, the BELS activities provide a strong reinforcement and practice of skills with an *end product,* illustrating the student's understanding of the skill. These products (e.g., word sorts, unscrambled words, etc.) assist the teacher in monitoring student performance at the literacy center and determining success with the particular skill. The *stages or levels of difficulty* section noted on each BELS activity provide a guide to teachers as they differentiate instruction and meet the specific skill needs of all of their students.

## TEACHING EFFECTIVELY

Teaching early literacy skills effectively requires that the teacher review with the students why the skills are important. Next the teacher provides examples that model or show children what they are expected to do, and last the teacher provides both supervised and independent opportunities for children to show that they understand and can use the skill or strategy. The *demonstrate, demonstrate, practice, and prove* teaching model is essential for effective teaching and critical for teaching early literacy skills.

First, the teacher should *demonstrate* the expected behavior. Next, students are given a chance to *demonstrate* their understanding. When students are actively engaged in doing this, the teacher should provide supportive feedback so they will know when they are doing it right or corrective feedback so they will know when they are doing it wrong and how to do it right. This step helps to ensure that children know what to do and that they don't practice skills or strategies incorrectly. It is an opportunity for the teacher to "check for understanding" before asking students to practice or perform independently. When the teacher is sure that all of the children have learned the skill, it is time to *practice* doing it "independently." To maximize the benefits of practice during "independent work time" (IWT), the teacher should:

- Provide supportive feedback so students know they are doing the behaviors correctly.
- Provide corrective feedback so students don't practice doing behaviors incorrectly.

This type of "guided practice" reduces errors because students perform under direction and with clear, specific feedback on their performance. After the teacher has shown students what to do (teacher demonstrates) and students have shown that they know what to do (students demonstrate) *and* can do it (students practice), the teacher should have students periodically *prove* that they have mastered the content by frequently checking for understanding and monitoring performance and progress.

## Letter Naming Fluency Content Preview

Assessments of letter naming fluency typically require that students are presented with upper- and lowercase letters arranged in random order and asked to name as many letters as they can. In DIBELS Letter Naming Fluency, students are considered at risk for difficulty achieving early literacy benchmark goals if they perform in the lowest 20% of students in their district and at some risk if they perform between the 20th and 40th percentile (Good & Kaminski, 2002). These students will profit from many of the activities in *Strategies and Lessons for Improving Basic Early Literacy Skills*.

## Initial Sound Fluency Content Preview

Assessments of initial sound fluency (ISF) require that the child is shown a set of pictures and then asked to identify (i.e., point to or mention) the one picture that begins with the sound produced by the teacher. For example, the teacher says, "This is sink, cat, gloves, and hat. Which of these begins with /s/?" and the child points to the correct picture. The child is also asked to orally produce the beginning sound for an orally presented word that matches one of the given pictures. The teacher keeps track of the amount of time taken to identify and produce the correct sound and converts the score into the number of initial sounds correct in a minute. The ISF measure takes about three minutes to administer and has over 20 alternate forms to monitor progress. On DIBELS

Initial Sound Fluency, the benchmark goal is 25 to 35 initial sounds correct by the middle of kindergarten. Students scoring below 10 initial sounds correct in the middle of kindergarten may need instructional support (Good & Kaminski, 2002). The activities in *Strategies and Lessons for Improving Basic Early Literacy Skills* will address these needs.

## Phoneme Segmentation Fluency Content Preview

Phoneme segmentation fluency (PSF) assessments evaluate the extent to which a child can orally divide a word into its individual sounds. For example, the teacher says, "sat," and the student says, "/s/ /a/ /t/" to receive three possible points for the word. After the student responds, the teacher presents the next word and so forth. The total number of correct phonemes produced in one minute determines the final score. Students scoring below 10 in the spring of kindergarten and fall of first grade may need instructional support to achieve benchmark goals (Good & Kaminski, 2002). Teachers will find that the activities in *Strategies and Lessons for Improving Basic Early Literacy Skills* will specifically address these student skill needs.

## Nonsense Word Fluency Content Preview

The nonsense word fluency (NWF) assessment identifies the student's knowledge of letters and sounds. The child is shown randomly ordered nonsense words (e.g., sig, rav, ov) and asked to produce verbally the individual sound of each letter in the word or to verbally produce, or read, the whole nonsense word. For example, if the stimulus word is "vaj" the student could say /v/ /a/ /j/ or say the word /vaj/ to obtain a total of three letter sounds correct. The benchmark goal for Nonsense Word Fluency is 50 correct letter sounds per minute by the middle of first grade. Students scoring below 30 in the middle of first grade may need instructional support to achieve first-grade reading goals (Good & Kaminski, 2002). These students will profit from activities in *Strategies and Lessons for Improving Basic Early Literacy Skills*.

## Oral Reading Fluency Content Preview

Oral reading fluency (ORF) is measured by having students read a grade level passage aloud for one minute. Words omitted, substituted, and hesitations of more than three seconds are scored as errors. Words self-corrected within three seconds are scored as accurate. The number of correct words per minute from the passage is the oral reading fluency rate. The benchmark goals are 40 in spring of first grade, 90 in spring of second grade, and 110 in spring of third grade. Students may need instructional support if they score below 10 in spring of first grade, below 50 in spring of second grade, and below 70 in spring of third grade; students scoring below 30 in the middle of first grade may need instructional support to achieve first-grade reading goals (Good & Kaminski, 2002). The activities in *Strategies and Lessons for Improving Basic Early Literacy Skills* will provide both fluency practice and guidance using short stories and nursery rhymes that emphasize reading with expression, appropriate phrasing and intonation.

## Teaching Early Literacy Skills

Reading is fundamental to success in our society and at the center of the latest federal, state, and local initiatives to improve education (Farstrup & Samuels, 2002; Goodman, 2006; Kuhn et al., 2006; International Reading Association, 2001, 2007; National Institute of Child Health and Human Development, 2000a, 2000b, 2000c; National Research Council, 1998; National Reading Panel, 2000; No Child Left Behind Act of 2001; Samuels & Farstrup, 2006; Vaughn & Briggs, 2003). The ability to read is highly valued and essential for academic, social, and economic advancement. Despite America's effective educational system, many children fail to read adequately by the end of third grade and large numbers of young people continue to struggle with reading and remain at risk in middle school, rarely performing at the same level as their more advantaged peers. Culturally and ethnically diverse learners who are struggling readers are also more likely to experience continuous failure, to be referred and placed in special education, to experience life in the lower track in school, and to enter the world after school as a high school dropout.

When questions arise about how best to teach reading skills, all fingers point in the direction of a few fundamental factors (International Reading Association, 2007; National Institute of Child Health and Human Development, 2000a, 2000b, 2000c). According to the Committee on the Prevention of Reading Difficulties in Young Children (Snow, Burns, & Griffin, 1998), these include (a) using reading to obtain meaning from print, (b) having frequent and intensive opportunities to read, (c) being exposed to frequent, regular spelling–sound relationships, (d) learning about the nature of the alphabetic writing system, and (e) understanding the structure of spoken words. Further, this group pointed out that adequate progress in learning to read beyond initial levels depended on:

- a working understanding of how sounds are represented alphabetically,
- sufficient practice in reading to achieve fluency with different kinds of text,
- sufficient background knowledge and vocabulary to render written texts meaningful and interesting,
- control over procedures for monitoring comprehension and repairing misunderstandings, and
- continued interest and motivation to read for a variety of purposes. (pp. 3–4)

Efforts to improve reading and literacy skills also must avoid some pitfalls to be effective:

There are three potential stumbling blocks that are known to throw children off course on the journey to skilled reading. The first obstacle, which arises at the outset of reading acquisition, is difficulty understanding and using the alphabetic principle—the idea that written spellings systematically represent spoken words. It is hard to comprehend connected text if word recognition is inaccurate or laborious. The second obstacle is a failure to transfer the comprehension skills of spoken language to reading and to acquire new strategies that may be specifically needed for reading. The third obstacle to reading will magnify the first two: the absence or loss of an initial motivation to read or failure to develop a mature appreciation of the rewards of reading. (Snow et al., 1998, pp. 4–5)

These critical factors, directions, and conclusions were supported by blue-ribbon panels (cf. National Institute of Child Health and Human Development, 2000a, 2000b, 2000c; National Research Council, 1998), and most literacy scholars agree that the majority of reading problems faced by children, adolescents, and young adults are the result of stumbling blocks, obstacles, and problems that should have been addressed during early elementary school years (cf. International Reading Association, 2007). To that end, *Strategies and Lessons for Improving Basic Early Literacy Skills* is a collection of lessons/activities to use in helping students remain actively engaged in critical tool skills that many believe are the foundation for literacy and academic achievement later in life.

## EARLY LITERACY INSTRUCTION IN PERSPECTIVE

The most successful teachers of reading implement appropriate instruction to teach literacy skills and strategies, evaluate the effectiveness of their lessons, and identify the students who need further practice with the skill or strategy taught. We know that even when students are receiving instruction in the concepts in which they are being assessed, some need more practice with particular skills. In an attempt to provide assistance with specific instruction in deficit areas, as identified on formal and informal assessments, we created lessons to extend those concepts for children. We did this with activities that teach concepts at their most basic levels, using a script with a four-step instructional presentation, providing examples of differentiation and scaffolding, and maximizing the use of instructional time. *Although the lessons are explicit, teachers we have worked with have personalized them while maintaining their overall purpose.*

Each lesson has the potential to be taught repeatedly, adjusting the materials as needed, until the skill/strategy is mastered. This gives opportunities to personalize the lessons to meet the needs of the students. We encourage you to use your own knowledge of literacy development to extend and enrich the lessons. We intentionally designed the lessons to have three stages of differentiation and, in some cases, sequenced the lessons specifically to scaffold instruction.

Knowing that the biggest issue facing teachers in the classroom today is time, our lessons were developed so that they may be implemented in under 15 minutes. In cases where the lessons required more time to complete, we intentionally separated them into parts. Finally, we provided a list of materials needed to teach the lesson and included black line masters for handouts and transparencies.

Although we have a suggested framework for including these lessons in the literacy block, you may find that they are also a valuable resource for use during transition times or when you find an extra 15 minutes in your schedule. They may also be used by literacy support teachers, tutors, and/or parents to reinforce concepts taught in the classroom.

## BUILDING EARLY LITERACY SKILLS

We have worked with many teachers who have used the activities in this book to help children develop critical early literacy skills. They have worked in small rural and large urban schools. Their students have come from the variety of cultural and linguistic backgrounds that are common in many districts across the nation. Their experiences have helped us improve the activities. Their work has also provided support for the effectiveness of using regular assessments to plan instruction. We share brief case illustrations of their work before presenting the letter naming fluency, initial sound fluency, phoneme segmentation fluency, nonsense word fluency, and oral reading fluency classroom activities in the sections that follow.

# 2

# Letter Naming
# Fluency

*If children do not know letter names and shapes, they need to be taught them along with phonemic awareness.*

National Institute for Literacy (2003)

Activities 1 and 2a–2e should be taught in sequential order. Activities 3–5 may be taught as separate lessons or as additional practice for letter identification and letter naming activities as part of regular reading lessons. Activity 1 helps children recognize the term "letter" as different from the terms "shape" and/or "number." Activities 2a–2e introduce different letter forms (e.g., "tall," "short circular," "short hump" letters) in an intentional and purposeful manner to promote successful discrimination and letter naming fluency. Activities 3–5 help children distinguish uppercase and lowercase letters.

## Improving Letter Naming Fluency

In Mr. Bristow's school, benchmark assessments are administered in kindergarten through third grade. At the beginning of the year, he reviewed the previous year scores for his first-grade students and identified six children at-risk on letter naming fluency. He looked at the scores for his class after the Fall Benchmark assessment and found that Juan, Jiban, Felix, and Carrie were not making adequate progress (see Table 2.1).

**Table 2.1** Benchmark

| | Benchmark | | | |
| | Kindergarten | | First | |
| Student | Beginning | Middle | End | Beginning |
|---------|-----------|--------|-----|-----------|
| Juan | 2 | 10 | 11 | 8* |
| Jiban | 17 | 12 | 11 | 14* |
| Manuel | 5 | 19 | 31 | 38 |
| Felix | 10 | 11 | 10 | 11* |
| Carrie | 7 | 14 | 20 | 21* |
| Monique | 6 | 23 | 34 | 37 |

NOTE: *Small-group skills instruction needed.

During small-group skills instructional time, Mr. Bristow worked with his teaching assistant to use Activities 2a–2e to help these students recognize and name the letters more fluently. At the end of each week, the children recorded their performance on a chart and Mr. Bristow sent home a copy of it with a note about their progress. As the year progressed and the students maintained their letter naming skills, they moved into different small groups for instruction and worked on other early literacy areas.

# Classroom Activities

## Activity 1: Distinguishing Between Letters and Non-Letters

Purpose: The learner will [TLW] distinguish between letters and non-letters in order to build a foundation for letter recognition.

Sample Standard Course of Study [SCOS] Competency Goal Objective:

TLW recognize and name uppercase and lowercase letters of the alphabet (adapted from *Language Arts: Kindergarten*, n.d.).

## Instructional Strategies

*Input/Modeling [Demonstrate]*

- Explain to the student(s) the purpose of the activity: **"Today we are going to sort letters and _____."** (shapes, numbers, etc.)
- Place Transparency 1 on the overhead.

**Table 2.2** Materials Needed for Instruction

## Grouping Strategies

| Whole Group | Small Group | Independent |
|---|---|---|
| Materials:<br><br>• Magnetic letters<br>• Overhead projector<br>• Various objects/shapes<br>• Magnetic numbers<br>• Overhead transparency TR1<br><br>*Optional:*<br><br>*Overhead transparencies of letters, numbers, objects/shapes, and words cut apart so they can be manipulated easily* | Materials:<br><br>• Magnetic letters<br>• Vertical magnetic surface that you can write on with chalk or dry erase marker<br>• Chalk or dry erase marker<br>• Eraser<br>• Various magnetic objects/shapes<br>• Magnetic numbers<br><br>*Optional:*<br><br>*Cards with letters, numbers, objects/shapes, and words for students to manipulate into groups* | Materials:<br><br>• Same objects as in whole/small-group activities<br>• Accountability sheet for students to record their work<br><br>*Optional:*<br><br>*Cut and paste sheet HO1*<br><br>*Scissors* |

- Place the five letters and five _____ (shapes, numbers, etc.) at the top of overhead transparency.
- Say: *"I am placing these at the top of my paper. Now I am going to sort them by putting all the letters in my circle."*
- As you begin to sort the objects, think aloud your sorting processes, *"Let's see, this one is on our [word wall/alphabet chart], so this is a letter. I will put this one in our circle. This one is a triangle. I know that is not a letter, so I will put it down here outside the circle."*
- Continue modeling using two more of the manipulatives.

*Guided Practice [Demonstrate]*

- With the final six manipulatives say: *"Now, I need your help. I am going to touch something and I need you to let me know if I should put it in the circle because it is a letter or leave it out of the circle because it is not a letter. If you believe it is a letter touch your nose. If you do not believe it is a letter, touch your ear."*
- Touch one of the objects and check the students for their responses.
- Call on a student with the correct answer to explain why the student chose that answer.
- Continue with the other manipulatives until all ten are sorted.

*Independent Practice [Practice]*

Before independent work time, explain the activity to students and demonstrate how they will complete an accountability sheet.

1. Precut the letters and circles at the bottom of the sheet and place them in plastic sandwich bags prior to the activity.

2. Place the manipulatives in your ABC center for students to practice the activity during independent work time.

3. Place accountability sheets (black line of Transparency 1) in the center for the students to record in the circle the letters they found in the group of manipulatives.

4. Have students complete the activity sheet by pasting the letters inside the circle and the shapes outside the circle.

*Check for Understanding [Prove]*

- As the students are actively responding, you should provide corrective and/or supportive feedback.
- Note the students who are still having difficulty for extra practice during independent work time.

## Differentiation

| Stage 1 | Stage 2 | Stage 3 |
|---------|---------|---------|
| Sort by two very different attributes. *Example:* letters and shapes or letters and objects. | Sort by two often-confused attributes. *Example:* letters and numbers and/or letters and words. | Sort by three or more attributes. *Example:* letters, numbers, AND shapes or letters, numbers, words, AND shapes. |

## Attachments

- Cut and paste activity sheet Handout 1.
- Overhead transparency/black line master Transparency 1.

# Transparency 1

**Letter Sort**

# Handout 1

## Letters

Name: _____     Date: _____

Place the cut-out pictures on the table beside the sheet. Sort the pictures into groups of *letters and "not-letters."* Paste the letters *in the circle* below. Paste the "not-letters" around the circle.

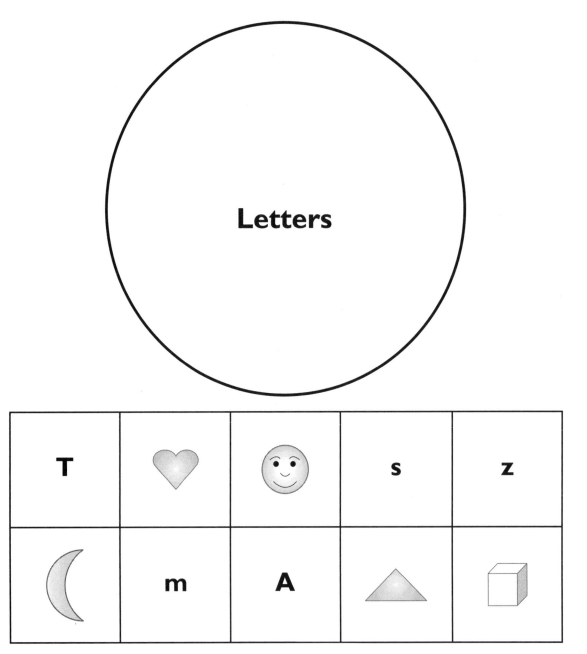

## Activity 2a: Distinguishing Letter Forms (Tall Letters)

Purpose: The learner will [TLW] distinguish between letter "forms" in order to build a foundation for letter recognition.

Sample Standard Course of Study [SCOS] Competency Goal Objective:

TLW recognize and name upper and lower case letters of the alphabet (adapted from *Language Arts: Kindergarten*, n.d.).

### Grouping Strategies

| Whole Group | Small Group | Independent |
|---|---|---|
| Materials: | Materials: | Materials: |
| • Magnetic letters | • Magnetic letters | • Same objects as in |
| • Overhead projector | • Vertical magnetic surface | whole/small-group activities |
| • Overhead transparency TR1 | you can write on with | • Accountability sheet for |
| • Chalkboard or dry erase | chalk or dry erase marker | students to record their |
| board | • Chalk or dry erase marker | work: TR1 |
| • Chalk or markers | • Eraser | |
| • Lines drawn on board as | | |
| example for letter formation | *Optional:* | *Optional:* |
| | | *Cut and paste sheet HO2a* |
| *Optional:* | *Cards with letters for students to* | *Scissors* |
| | *manipulate into groups* | |
| *Overhead transparency letters* | | |

## Instructional Strategies

*Input/Modeling [Demonstrate]*

- Explain to the student(s) the purpose of the activity: "***Today we are going to sort letters by their 'shape' or 'form.'***"
- Place Transparency 1 on the overhead.
- Place the letters t, h, l, f, b, and k in the top box of the overhead transparency.
- Say: "***I am placing these at the top of my paper. I chose these letters because they all are 'tall' letters. I know they are all 'tall' letters because when I write these letters, I always begin at the top line of my paper.***"
- Go to the chalk/dry erase board and demonstrate how each letter is formed: "***Let me show you what I mean. I am going to write the letter 't' on our board. I always begin by placing my marker on the top line and go straight down to the bottom line. Next, I place a small straight line on the middle line and there I have my lowercase 't.'***"
- Continue modeling using two more of the letter examples.

*Guided Practice [Demonstrate]*

- Now take those letters and mix in the letters o, s, z, m, and c: "***Now, I need your help. I have mixed in some other letters that are not 'tall' letters.***

*I am going to touch one of them and I need you to let me know if I should put it in the circle because it is a tall letter or leave it out of the circle because it is not a tall letter. If you believe it is a tall letter, touch your nose. If you do not believe it is a tall letter, touch your toes."*

- Touch one of the letters and check the students for their responses.
- Call on a student with the correct answer to explain why the student chose that answer.
- Continue with the other manipulatives until all 11 are sorted.

*Independent Practice [Practice]*

Before independent work time, explain the activity to students and demonstrate how they will complete an accountability sheet.

1. Place the manipulatives in your ABC center for students to practice the activity during independent work time.
   - Place accountability sheets (black line of Transparency 1) in the center for the students to record in the circle the letters they found in the group of manipulatives.

2. Students will complete the activity sheet, Handout 2a, by pasting (or writing) the tall letters inside the circle and the short letters outside the circle.
   - Precut the letters at the bottom of the sheet and place them in plastic sandwich bags prior to the activity.

*Check for Understanding [Prove]*

- As the students are actively responding, you should provide corrective and/or supportive feedback.
- Note the students who are still having difficulty for extra practice during independent work time.

## Attachments

- Overhead transparency/black line master Transparency 1.
- Cut and paste activity sheet Handout 2a.

### Differentiation

| Stage 1 | Stage 2 | Stage 3 |
|---------|---------|---------|
| Sort by two very different attributes. *Example:* tall letters and short letters. (t, h, l, f, b, k, o, s, z, m, c) | Sort by two semiconfusing attributes. *Example:* tall letters and hanging letters, circle letters and hump letters, or short stick letters and short hump letters. (g, p, q, t, h, l, f, b, k, y, j) OR (o, c, e, a, s, m, n, u, r) OR (w, x, v, z, i, m, n, u, r) | Sort letters and explain their own reasons they sorted the letters the way they did. |

# Handout 2a

## Tall Letters

Name: _____          Date: _____

Place the cut-out letters on the table beside the sheet. Sort them into two groups, tall letters and "not-tall letters." Paste the tall letters in the circle below. Paste the "not-tall letters" around the circle.

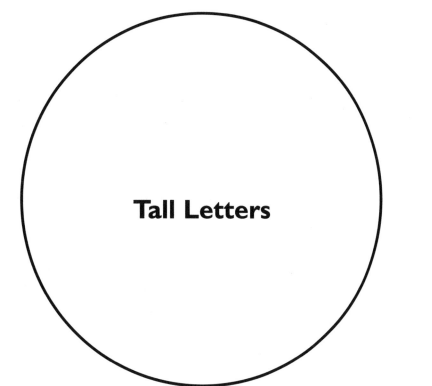

**Tall Letters**

| t | r | f | n | K |
|---|---|---|---|---|
| u | l | h | b | m |

## Activity 2b: Distinguishing Letter Forms (Short Circular Letters)

Purpose: The learner will [TLW] distinguish between letter "forms" in order to build a foundation for letter recognition.

Sample Standard Course of Study [SCOS] Competency Goal Objective:

TLW recognize and name uppercase and lowercase letters of the alphabet (adapted from *Language Arts: Kindergarten*, n.d.).

### Grouping Strategies

| Whole Group | Small Group | Independent |
|---|---|---|
| Materials: | Materials: | Materials: |
| • Magnetic letters<br>• Overhead projector<br>• Overhead transparency TR1<br>• Chalkboard or dry erase board<br>• Chalk or markers<br>• Lines drawn on board as example for letter formation<br><br>*Optional:*<br><br>*Overhead transparency letters* | • Magnetic letters<br>• Vertical magnetic surface you can write on with chalk or dry erase marker<br>• Chalk or dry erase marker<br>• Eraser<br><br>*Optional:*<br><br>*Cards with letters for students to manipulate into groups* | • Same objects as in whole/small-group activities<br>• Accountability sheet for students to record their work: TR1<br><br>*Optional:*<br><br>*Cut and paste sheet HO2b*<br><br>*Scissors* |

### Instructional Strategies

*Input/Modeling [Demonstrate]*

- Explain to the student(s) the purpose of the activity: ***"Today we are again going to sort letters by their 'shape' or 'form.'"***
- Place Transparency 1 on the overhead
- Place the letters o, c, e, a, and s in the top box of the overhead transparency.
- Say: ***"I am placing these at the top of my paper. I chose these letters because they all are 'short circular' letters. I know they are all 'short circular' letters because when I write these letters, I always begin at the middle line of my paper and curve to the left just like I was making a circle."***
- Go to the chalk/dry erase board and demonstrate how each letter is formed: ***"Let me show you what I mean. I am going to write the letter 'o' on our board. I always begin by placing my marker just below the middle line. Next, I curve my marker around to the left to finish the 'o.'"***
- Continue modeling using two more of the letter examples.

*Guided Practice [Demonstrate]*

- ***Now take those letters and mix in the letters t, w, p, j, and u: "Now, I need your help. I have mixed in some other letters that are not 'short*** *circular' letters. I am going to touch one of them, and I need you to let me know if I should put it in the circle because it is a short circular letter or leave it out of the circle because it is not a short circular letter. If you believe it is a short circular letter, touch your chin. If you do not believe it is a tall letter, touch your belly."*

- Touch one of the letters and check the students for their responses.
- Call on a student with the correct answer to explain why the student chose that answer.
- Continue with the other manipulatives until all ten are sorted.

*Independent Practice [Practice]*

Before independent work time, explain the activity to students and demonstrate how they will complete an accountability sheet.

1. Place the manipulatives in your ABC center for students to practice the activity during independent work time.
   - Place accountability sheets (black line of Transparency 1) in the center for the students to record in the circle the letters they found in the group of manipulatives.

2. Students will complete the activity sheet, Handout 2b, by pasting (or writing) the short circular letters inside the circle and the other letters outside the circle.
   - Precut the letters at the bottom of the sheet and place them in plastic sandwich bags prior to the activity.

*Check for Understanding [Prove]*

- As the students are actively responding, you should provide corrective and/or supportive feedback.
- Note the students who are still having difficulty for extra practice during independent work time.

**Attachment**

- Cut and paste activity sheet Handout 2b.

## Differentiation (Short circular letters)

| Stage 1 | Stage 2 | Stage 3 |
|---------|---------|---------|
| Sort by two very different attributes. *Example:* tall letters and short letters. (t, h, l, f, b, k, o, s, z, m, c) | Sort by two semiconfusing attributes. *Example:* tall letters and hanging letters, circle letters and hump letters, or short stick letters and short hump letters. (g, p, q, t, h, l, f, b, k, y, j) OR (o, c, e, a, s, m, n, u, r) OR (w, x, v, z, i, m, n, u, r) | Sort letters and explain their own reasons they sorted the letters the way they did. |

# Handout 2b

## Short Circular Letters

Name: _____     Date: _____

Place the cut-out pictures on the table beside the sheet. Sort them into two groups, short circular letters and "not-short circular letters." Paste the short circular letters in the circle below. Paste the "not-short circular letters" around the circle.

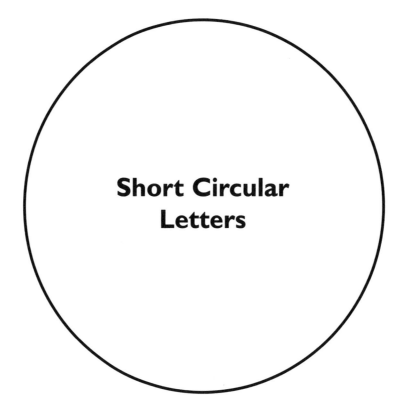

**Short Circular Letters**

| t | c | b | a | d |
|---|---|---|---|---|
| o | l | e | k | s |

# Activity 2c: Distinguishing Letter Forms (Short Stick Letters)

Purpose: The learner will [TLW] distinguish between letter "forms" in order to build a foundation for letter recognition.

Sample Standard Course of Study [SCOS] Competency Goal Objective:

TLW recognize and name uppercase and lowercase letters of the alphabet (adapted from *Language Arts: Kindergarten*, n.d.).

## Grouping Strategies

| Whole Group | Small Group | Independent |
|---|---|---|
| Materials:<br><br>• Magnetic letters<br>• Overhead projector<br>• Overhead transparency TR1<br>• Chalkboard or dry erase board<br>• Chalk or markers<br>• Lines drawn on board as example for letter formation<br><br>*Optional:*<br><br>*Overhead transparency letters* | Materials:<br><br>• Magnetic letters<br>• Vertical magnetic surface you can write on with chalk or dry erase marker<br>• Chalk or dry erase marker<br>• Eraser<br><br>*Optional:*<br><br>*Cards with letters for students to manipulate into groups* | Materials:<br><br>• Same objects as in whole/small-group activities<br>• Accountability sheet for students to record their work: TR1<br><br>*Optional:*<br><br>*Cut and paste sheet HO2c*<br><br>*Scissors* |

## Instructional Strategies

### Input/Modeling [Demonstrate]

- Explain to the student(s) the purpose of the activity: **"Today we are again going to sort letters by their 'shape' or 'form.'"**
- Place Transparency 1 on the overhead.
- Place the letters w, x, v, z, and i in the top box of the overhead transparency.
- Say: **"I am placing these at the top of my paper. I chose these letters because they all are 'short stick' letters. I know they are all 'short stick' letters because when I write these letters, I always begin at the middle line of my paper and make a straight or slanted line down to end at the bottom line."**
- Go to the chalk/dry erase board and demonstrate how each letter is formed: **"Let me show you what I mean. I am going to write the letter 'w' on our board. I always begin by placing my marker on the middle line. Next, I draw a slant line down to the bottom line. Then I do the same thing with different straight slants three more times until I have written the letter 'w.'"**
- Continue modeling using two more of the letter examples.

### Guided Practice [Demonstrate]

- Now take those letters and mix in the letters t, s, p, j, and u: **"Now, I need your help. I have mixed in some other letters that are not 'short stick'** *letters. I am going to touch one of them, and I need you to let me know if I should put it in the circle because it is a short stick letter or leave it out of the circle because it is not a short stick letter. If you believe it is a short stick letter, touch your chin. If you do not believe it is a short stick letter, touch your belly."*

- Touch one of the letters and check the students for their responses.
- Call on a student with the correct answer to explain why the student chose that answer.
- Continue with the other manipulatives until all ten are sorted.

*Independent Practice [Practice]*

Before independent work time, explain the activity to students and demonstrate how they will complete an accountability sheet.

1. Place the manipulatives in your ABC center for students to practice the activity during independent work time.
   - Place accountability sheets (black line of Transparency 1) in the center for the students to record in the circle the letters they found in the group of manipulatives.

2. Students will complete the activity sheet, Handout 2c, by pasting (or writing) the short stick letters inside the circle and the other letters outside the circle.
   - Precut the letters at the bottom of the sheet and place them in plastic sandwich bags prior to the activity.

*Check for Understanding [Prove]*

- As the students are actively responding, you should provide corrective and/or supportive feedback.
- Note the students who are still having difficulty for extra practice during independent work time.

**Attachment**

- Cut and paste activity sheet Handout 2c.

### Differentiation

| Stage 1 | Stage 2 | Stage 3 |
|---|---|---|
| Sort by two very different attributes. *Example:* tall letters and short letters. (t, h, l, f, b, k, o, s, z, m, c) | Sort by two semiconfusing attributes. *Example:* tall letters and hanging letters, circle letters and hump letters, or short stick letters and short hump letters. (g, p, q, t, h, l, f, b, k, y, j) OR (o, c, e, a, s, m, n, u, r) OR (w, x, v, z, i, m, n, u, r) | Sort letters and explain their own reasons they sorted the letters the way they did. |

# Handout 2c

## Short Stick Letters

Name: _____     Date: _____

Place the cut-out letters on the table beside the sheet. Sort them into two groups, short stick letters and "not-short stick letters." Paste the short stick letters in the circle below. Paste the "not-short stick letters" around the circle.

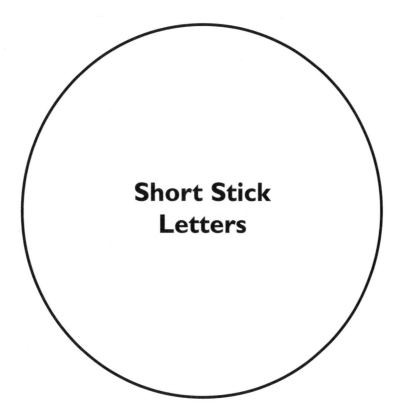

| w | d | x | e | z |
|---|---|---|---|---|
| a | v | f | i | h |

# Activity 2d: Distinguishing Letter Forms (Short Hump Letters)

Purpose: The learner will [TLW] distinguish between letter "forms" in order to build a foundation for letter recognition.

Sample Standard Course of Study [SCOS] Competency Goal Objective:

TLW recognize and name uppercase and lowercase letters of the alphabet (adapted from *Language Arts: Kindergarten*, n.d.).

## Grouping Strategies (Short hump letters)

| Whole Group | Small Group | Independent |
|---|---|---|
| Materials:<br><br>• Magnetic letters<br>• Overhead projector<br>• Overhead transparency TR1<br>• Chalkboard or dry erase board<br>• Chalk or markers<br>• Lines drawn on board as example for letter formation<br><br>*Optional:*<br><br>*Overhead transparency letters* | Materials:<br><br>• Magnetic letters<br>• Vertical magnetic surface you can write on with chalk or dry erase marker<br>• Chalk or dry erase marker<br>• Eraser<br><br>*Optional:*<br><br>*Cards with letters for students to manipulate into groups* | Materials:<br><br>• Same objects as in whole/small-group activities<br>• Accountability sheet for students to record their work: TR1<br><br>*Optional:*<br><br>*Cut and paste sheet HO2d*<br>*Scissors* |

## Instructional Strategies:

*Input/Modeling [Demonstrate]*

- Explain to the student(s) the purpose of the activity: ***"Today we are again going to sort letters by their 'shape' or 'form.'"***
- Place Transparency 1 on the overhead.
- Place the letters m, u, n, and r in the top box of the overhead transparency.
- Say: ***"I am placing these at the top of my paper. I chose these letters because they all are 'short hump' letters. I know they are all 'short hump' letters because when I write these letters, I always begin at the middle line of my paper. These letters all have a short straight line down to end at the bottom line and make a 'hump.'"***
- Go to the chalk/dry erase board and demonstrate how each letter is formed: ***"Let me show you what I mean. I am going to write the letter 'm' on our board. I always begin by placing my marker on the middle line. Next, I draw a straight line down to the bottom line. Then I make my hump line and one more hump line to create the letter 'm.'"***
- Continue modeling using two more of the letter examples.

*Guided Practice [Demonstrate]*

- Now take those letters and mix in the letters x, e, i, z, d, and f: ***"Now, I need your help. I have mixed in some other letters that are not 'short*** *hump' letters. I am going to touch one of them, and I need you to let me know if I should put it in the circle because it is a short hump letter or leave it out of the circle because it is not a short hump letter. If you believe it is a short hump letter, touch your chin. If you do not believe it is a short hump letter, touch your belly."*

- Touch one of the letters and check the students for their responses.
- Call on a student with the correct answer to explain why the student chose that answer.
- Continue with the other manipulatives until all ten are sorted.

*Independent Practice [Practice]*

Before independent work time, explain the activity to students and demonstrate how they will complete an accountability sheet.

1. Place the manipulatives in your ABC center for students to practice the activity during independent work time.
   - Place accountability sheets (black line of Transparency 1) in the center for the students to record in the circle the letters they found in the group of manipulatives.

2. Students will complete the activity sheet, Handout 2d, by pasting (or writing) the short hump letters inside the circle and the other letters outside the circle.
   - Precut the letters at the bottom of the sheet and place them in plastic sandwich bags prior to the activity.

*Check for Understanding [Prove]*

- As the students are actively responding, you should provide corrective and/or supportive feedback.
- Note the students who are still having difficulty for extra practice during independent work time.

## Attachment

- Cut and paste activity sheet Handout 2d.

## Differentiation

| Stage 1 | Stage 2 | Stage 3 |
|---------|---------|---------|
| Sort by two very different attributes. *Example:* tall letters and short letters. (t, h, l, f, b, k, o, s, z, m, c) | Sort by two semiconfusing attributes. *Example:* tall letters and hanging letters, circle letters and hump letters, or short stick letters and short hump letters. (g, p, q, t, h, l, f, b, k, y, j) OR (o, c, e, a, s, m, n, u, r) OR (w, x, v, z, i, m, n, u, r) | Sort letters and explain their own reasons they sorted the letters the way they did. |

# Handout 2d

## Short Hump Letters

Name: _____     Date: _____

Place the cut-out letters on the table beside the sheet. Sort them into two groups, short hump letters and "not-short hump letters." Paste the short hump letters in the circle below. Paste the "not-short hump letters" around the circle.

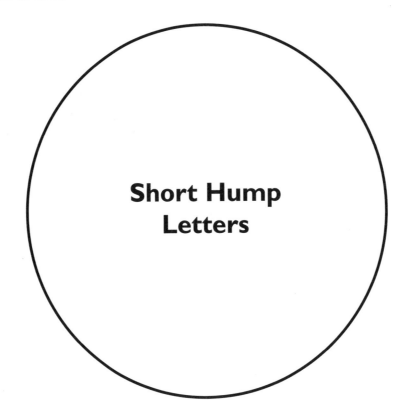

| u | d | n | e | z |
|---|---|---|---|---|
| a | m | f | i | r |

## Activity 2e: Distinguishing Letter Forms (Hanging Letters)

Purpose: The learner will [TLW] distinguish between letter "forms" in order to build a foundation for letter recognition.

Sample Standard Course of Study [SCOS] Competency Goal Objective:

TLW recognize and name uppercase and lowercase letters of the alphabet (adapted from *Language Arts: Kindergarten*, n.d.).

### Grouping Strategies (Hanging letters)

| Whole Group | Small Group | Independent |
|---|---|---|
| Materials: | Materials: | Materials: |
| • Magnetic letters<br>• Overhead projector<br>• Overhead transparency TR1<br>• Chalkboard or dry erase board<br>• Chalk or markers<br>• Lines drawn on board as example for letter formation | • Magnetic letters<br>• Vertical magnetic surface you can write on with chalk or dry erase marker<br>• Chalk or dry erase marker<br>• Eraser | • Same objects as in whole/small-group activities<br>• Accountability sheet for students to record their work: TR1 |
| *Optional:* | *Optional:* | *Optional:* |
| *Overhead transparency letters* | *Cards with letters for students to manipulate into groups* | *Cut and paste sheet HO2e*<br>*Scissors* |

## Instructional Strategies

*Input/Modeling [Demonstrate]*

- Explain to the student(s) the purpose of the activity: ***"Today we are again going to sort letters by their 'shape' or 'form.'"***
- Place Transparency 1 on the overhead.
- Place the letters y, g, p, j, and q in the top box of the overhead transparency.
- Say: ***"I am placing these at the top of my paper. I chose these letters because they all are 'hanging' letters. I know they are all 'hanging' letters because when I write these letters, I always go from the middle line of my paper and past the bottom line to write these letters."***
- Go to the chalk/dry erase board and demonstrate how each letter is formed: ***"Let me show you what I mean. I am going to write the letter 'y' on our board. I always begin by placing my marker on the middle line. Next, I draw a slant-straight line down to the bottom line. Then I go back up to the middle line and draw a slant line straight down past the bottom line to finish my letter 'y.'"***
- Continue modeling using two more of the letter examples.

*Guided Practice [Demonstrate]*

- Now take those letters and mix in the letters r, e, i, z, and f: ***"Now, I need your help. I have mixed in some other letters that are not 'hanging'*** *letters. I am going to touch one of them, and I need you to let me know if I should put it in the circle because it is a hanging letter or leave it out of the circle because it is not a hanging letter. If you believe it is a hanging letter, touch your chin. If you do not believe it is a hanging letter, touch your belly."*

- Touch one of the letters and check the students for their responses.
- Call on a student with the correct answer to explain why the student chose that answer.
- Continue with the other manipulatives until all ten are sorted.

*Independent Practice [Practice]*

Before independent work time, explain the activity to students and demonstrate how they will complete an accountability sheet.

1. Place the manipulatives in your ABC center for students to practice the activity during independent work time.
   - Place accountability sheets (black line of Transparency 1) in the center for the students to record in the circle the letters they found in the group of manipulatives.

2. Students will complete the activity sheet, Handout 2e, by pasting (or writing) the hanging letters inside the circle and the other letters outside the circle.
   - Precut the letters at the bottom of the sheet and place them in plastic sandwich bags prior to the activity.

*Check for Understanding [Prove]*

- As the students are actively responding, you should provide corrective and/or supportive feedback.
- Note the students who are still having difficulty for extra practice during independent work time.

**Attachment**

- Cut and paste activity sheet Handout 2e.

## Differentiation

| Stage 1 | Stage 2 | Stage 3 |
| --- | --- | --- |
| Sort by two very different attributes. *Example:* tall letters and short letters. (t, h, l, f, b, k, o, s, z, m, c) | Sort by two semi-confusing attributes. *Example:* tall letters and hanging letters, circle letters and hump letters, or short stick letters and short hump letters. (g, p, q, t, h, l, f, b, k, y, j) OR (o, c, e, a, s, m, n, u, r) OR (w, x, v, z, i, m, n, u, r) | Sort letters and explain their own reasons they sorted the letters the way they did. |

# Handout 2e

## Hanging Letters

Name: _____     Date: _____

Place the cut-out letters on the table beside the sheet. Sort them into two groups, hanging letters and "not-hanging letters." Paste the hanging letters in the circle below. Paste the "not-hanging letters" around the circle.

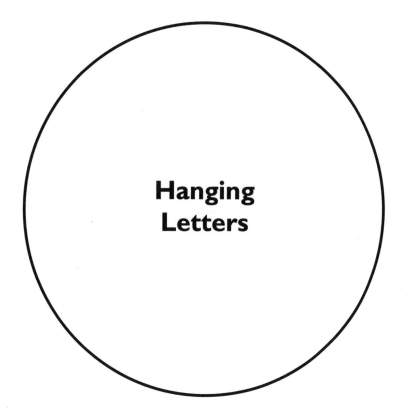

| y | w | q | e | p |
|---|---|---|---|---|
| a | g | f | j | r |

Activity 3: Distinguishing Same and Different Letters

Purpose: The learner will [TLW] distinguish between "same" letters and letters that are different in order to build a foundation for letter recognition.

Sample Standard Course of Study [SCOS] Competency Goal Objective:

TLW recognize and name uppercase and lowercase letters of the alphabet (adapted from *Language Arts: Kindergarten*, n.d.).

## Grouping Strategies

| Whole Group | Small Group | Independent |
|---|---|---|
| Materials:<br><br>• Magnetic letters with different fonts (uppercase and lowercase)<br>• Overhead projector<br>• Overhead transparency TR1<br><br>*Optional:*<br><br>*Overhead transparencies of letters using different fonts and cut apart so they can be manipulated easily* | Materials:<br><br>• Magnetic letters with different fonts (uppercase and lowercase)<br>• Vertical magnetic surface you can write on with chalk or dry erase marker<br>• Chalk or dry erase marker<br>• Eraser<br><br>*Optional:*<br><br>*Cards with letters with different fonts for students to manipulate* | Materials:<br><br>• Same objects as in whole/small-group activities<br>• Accountability sheet for students to record their work: TR1<br><br>*Optional:*<br><br>*Paper letters of different fonts cut apart and placed in plastic sandwich bags*<br><br>*HO3 handouts*<br><br>*Glue* |

## Instructional Strategies [may be adapted as new letters are introduced in adopted commercial reading program lessons]

*Input/Modeling [Demonstrate]*

- Explain to student(s) the purpose of the activity: ***"Today we are going to sort for the letter _____."***
- Review the attributes for the letter _____ by saying: ***"I know the letter _____ is a (tall, short, circle, curved . . . ) letter. I can find it on our sound/spelling cards here above our board."***
- Locate the letter on the sound/spelling cards and talk about its shape very explicitly.
- Say: ***"I know that sometimes when I see the letter _____ in other places, it sometimes has a little different shape, but I know it is still the letter _____."***

- Find the letter in a different font in your classroom and discuss how you know it is the same letter.
- Place Transparency 1 on the overhead.
- Place the five letter _____'s and five other letters at the top of the overhead transparency.
- Say: ***"I am placing these at the top of my paper. Now I am going to sort them by putting all the letter _____'s in my circle."***
- As you begin to sort the objects, think aloud your sorting processes: ***"Let's see, this one has (a tall stick, two curves, a circle/stick, etc.), so this is the letter _____. I will put this one in our circle. This one is shaped different. It does not (curve, have a tall stick, have a circle/stick, etc.). I know that this one is not the letter _____, so I will put it down here outside the circle."***
- Continue modeling using two more of the manipulatives.

### Guided Practice [Demonstrate]

- With the final six manipulatives say: ***"Now, I need your help. I am going to touch one of them, and I need you to let me know if I should put it in the circle because it is a letter _____ or leave it out of the circle because it is not a letter _____."***
- If you believe it is a letter, touch your nose. If you do not believe it is a letter, touch your ear.
- Touch one of the objects and check the students for their responses.
- Call on a student with the correct answer to explain why the student chose that answer.
- Continue with the other manipulatives until all ten are sorted.

### Independent Practice [Practice]

Before independent work time, explain the activity to students and demonstrate how they will complete an accountability sheet.

1. Place the manipulatives in your ABC center for students to practice the activity during independent work time.
   - Place accountability sheets (black line of Transparency 1) in the center for the students to record in the circle the letters they found in the group of manipulatives.

2. Students will complete the activity sheet by pasting the letter _____ inside the circle and the other letters outside the circle.
   - Precut the letters and circles at the bottom of the sheet and place them in plastic sandwich bags prior to the activity.

### Check for Understanding [Prove]

- As the students are actively responding, you should provide corrective and/or supportive feedback.
- Note the students who are still having difficulty for extra practice during independent work time.

## Differentiation

| Stage 1 | Stage 2 | Stage 3 |
|---------|---------|---------|
| Sort by two very different attributes. *Example:* if the letter introduced is the letter "s," use "tall" letters and "stick" letters that are not visually similar. (T, M, v, H, h, L . . .) | Sort by two semi-confusing attributes. *Example:* letters which are tall with letters which have tails. (h, y, t, j, f . . .) | Sort by letters that are sometimes confused by students. *Example:* letters which have similar shapes and are easily confused. (B, D, P/ b, d, p, q/ u, n, m/s, z/. . .) |

## Attachments

- Overhead transparency/black line master Transparency 1.
- Cut and paste any one of the activity sheet Handouts 3a–3e.

# Handout 3a

## Letters Revisited

Name: _____     Date: _____

Place the cut-out letters on the table beside the sheet. Sort them into two groups, letter _____ and "not-letter"_____. Paste the letter _____ in the circle below. Paste the "not-letters"_____ around the circle.

**Letters**

| | | | | |
|---|---|---|---|---|
| | | | | |
| | | | | |

# Handout 3b

## Letter Template 1: Century Gothic

| a | b | c | d | e | f |
|---|---|---|---|---|---|
| g | h | i | j | k | l |
| m | n | o | p | q | r |
| s | t | u | v | w | x |
| y | z |   |   |   |   |
| A | B | C | D | E | F |
| G | H | I | J | K | L |
| M | N | O | P | Q | R |
| S | T | U | V | W | X |
| Y | Z |   |   |   |   |

# Handout 3c

## Letter Template 2: Times New Roman

| | | | | | |
|---|---|---|---|---|---|
| a | b | c | d | e | f |
| g | h | i | j | k | l |
| m | n | o | p | q | r |
| s | t | u | v | w | x |
| y | z | | | | |
| A | B | C | D | E | F |
| G | H | I | J | K | L |
| M | N | O | P | Q | R |
| S | T | U | V | W | X |
| Y | Z | | | | |

# Handout 3d

## Letter Template 3: Comic Sans Serif

| a | b | c | d | e | f |
|---|---|---|---|---|---|
| g | h | i | j | k | l |
| m | n | o | p | q | r |
| s | t | u | v | w | x |
| y | z |   |   |   |   |
| A | B | C | D | E | F |
| G | H | I | J | K | L |
| M | N | O | P | Q | R |
| S | T | U | V | W | X |
| Y | Z |   |   |   |   |

# Handout 3e

## Letter Template 4: Bookman Old Style

| | | | | | |
|---|---|---|---|---|---|
| a | b | c | d | e | f |
| g | h | i | j | k | l |
| m | n | o | p | q | r |
| s | t | u | v | w | x |
| y | z | | | | |
| A | B | C | D | E | F |
| G | H | I | J | K | L |
| M | N | O | P | Q | R |
| S | T | U | V | W | X |
| Y | Z | | | | |

## Activity 4a: Distinguishing Uppercase and Lowercase Letters

Purpose: The learner will [TLW] distinguish between uppercase letters and lowercase letters in order to build a foundation for letter recognition.

Sample Standard Course of Study [SCOS] Competency Goal Objective:

TLW recognize and name uppercase and lowercase letters of the alphabet (adapted from *Language Arts: Kindergarten*, n.d.).

### Instructional Strategies [may be adapted as new letters are introduced in your reading program]

*Input/Modeling [Demonstrate]*

- Explain to the student(s) the purpose of the activity: ***"Today we are going to sort for uppercase and lowercase letter matches."***
- Review the attributes for the lowercase letters by saying: ***"I know the lowercase letters are found on our sound/spelling cards. I can find them on our sound/spelling cards here above our board."*** Point to the cards. ***"And if we look at _____ (our alphabet chart, word wall, etc.), we can see that we have both the uppercase and lowercase letters matched already."*** Point to the letter pairs displayed in your room. ***"The uppercase letters can usually be found on the left and the lowercase letters can usually be found on the right when you see them matched in pairs. Does anyone else have a way that we might know if a letter is an uppercase letter or a lowercase letter?"*** Validate the student's appropriate responses and clarify as needed.
- Place Transparency 4a on the overhead.

### Grouping Strategies

| Whole Group | Small Group | Independent |
|---|---|---|
| Materials: | Materials: | Materials: |
| • Magnetic letters with different fonts (uppercase and lowercase)<br>• Overhead projector<br>• Overhead transparency TR4a | • Magnetic letters with different fonts (uppercase and lowercase)<br>• Vertical magnetic surface you can write on with chalk or dry erase marker<br>• Chalk or dry erase marker<br>• Eraser | • Same objects as in whole/small-group activities<br>• Accountability sheet for students to record their work: TR4a |
| *Optional:*<br><br>*Overhead transparencies of letters using different fonts and cut apart so they can be manipulated easily* | *Optional:*<br><br>*Cards with letters with different fonts for students to manipulate* | *Optional:*<br><br>*Paper letters of different fonts cut apart and placed in plastic sandwich bags*<br>*HO4a*<br>*Glue* |

- Place the five letter pairs at the top of the overhead transparency (Aa, Dd, Mm, Ss, Pp).
- Say: ***"I am placing these letters at the top of my paper. Now I am going to sort them by putting all the uppercase letters in the left column and the lowercase match in the right column."***
- As you begin to sort the letters, think aloud your sorting processes: ***"Let's see, first I will find an uppercase letter. I know this one is an uppercase letter because it is a tall letter and I found it here on our chart on the left side. I will put this one in the left column. Now I will check my chart and look for its match."*** Locate the lowercase letter on your chart. ***"Here is the match, so now I need to find it in my magnetic letters. Here it is, so I will place it here beside its match in the right-hand column."***
- Continue modeling using two more of the manipulatives.

### Guided Practice [Demonstrate]

- With the final six manipulatives say, ***"Now, I need your help. I am going to touch one of them, and I need you to let me know if I should put it in the left column because it is an uppercase letter, or put it in the right column because it is the lowercase match."***
- "First, let's sort for all the uppercase letters.
- ***"If you believe it is an uppercase letter, touch your nose. If you do not believe it is an uppercase letter, touch your ear."***
- Touch one of the objects and check the students for their responses.
- Call on a student with the correct answer to explain why the student chose that answer.
- Place the letter in the left column and continue until the next three uppercase letters are identified.
- ***"Now we need to find the lowercase matches for these letters. If you believe it is a lowercase match, touch your chin. If it is not a match, touch your foot."***
- Touch one of the objects and check the students for their responses.
- Call on a student with the correct answer to explain why the student chose that answer.
- Place the letter in the right column and continue until the next three lowercase letters are matched with their uppercase letter.

### Independent Practice [Practice]

Before independent work time, explain the activity to students and demonstrate how they will complete an accountability sheet.

1. Place the manipulatives in your ABC center for students to practice the activity during independent work time.
   - Place accountability sheets (black line of Transparency 4a) in the center for the students to record in the columns the letters pairs they found in their group of manipulatives.

2. Students will complete the activity sheet, Handout 4a, by pasting the uppercase letters in the left column and the lowercase letter matches in the right column.

- Precut *five letter pairs* from the sheet provided and place them in plastic sandwich bags prior to the activity.

*Check for Understanding [Prove]*

- As the students are actively responding, you should provide corrective and/or supportive feedback.
- Note the students who are still having difficulty for extra practice during independent work time.

## Attachments

- Overhead transparency/black line master Transparency 4a.
- Cut and paste activity sheet Handout 4a.

### Differentiation

| Stage 1 | Stage 2 | Stage 3 |
|---------|---------|---------|
| Follow the above procedures and gradually add letter pairs to the original group until all letter pairs are introduced. | Follow the above procedures and introduce the script "a," script "g," and other script letters. | Follow the above procedures, but prepare letters and add letters that have no match or more than one match. For example, use the letters Vv, Ggg, Aaa, Dd **OR** Cc, Mm, Rr, K, I |

# Transparency 4a

## Uppercase and Lowercase Letter Match

| Uppercase Letters | Lowercase Letter Match |
|---|---|
|  |  |
|  |  |
|  |  |
|  |  |
|  |  |

# Handout 4a

## Uppercase and Lowercase Letter Match

Name: _____     Date: _____

Place the cut-out letters on the table beside the sheet. Sort them into two groups, uppercase letters and lowercase letters. Paste the uppercase letters in the left column. Paste the lowercase letter in the right column beside its match.

| Uppercase Letters | Lowercase Letter Match |
|---|---|
|  |  |
|  |  |
|  |  |
|  |  |
|  |  |

Activity 4b: Distinguishing Uppercase and Lowercase Letters (Using American Sign Language)

Purpose: The learner will [TLW] distinguish between uppercase letters and lowercase letters in order to build a foundation for letter recognition.

Sample Standard Course of Study [SCOS] Competency Goal Objective:

TLW recognize and name uppercase and lowercase letters of the alphabet (adapted from Language Arts: Kindergarten, n.d.).

## Grouping Strategies

| Whole Group | Small Group | Independent |
|---|---|---|
| Materials: <br><br>• Poster with American Sign Language hand signs for the alphabet <br>• Overhead projector <br>• Overhead transparency TR4b | Materials: <br><br>• Poster with American Sign Language hand signs for the alphabet <br>• Student copies of the American Sign Language hand signs for the alphabet | Materials: <br><br>• Same objects as in whole/small-group activities <br>• Accountability sheet for students to record their work: TR4b <br><br>*Optional:* <br><br>*Paper letters and hand signs cut apart and placed in plastic sandwich bags* <br>*HO4b* <br>*Glue* |

## Instructional Strategies [may be adapted as new letters are introduced in core reading program lessons]

*Input/Modeling [Demonstrate]*

- Explain to the student(s) the purpose of the activity: ***"Today we are going to use American Sign Language (ASL) to 'sign' the letters of the alphabet."***
- Show the poster and explain the purpose for the development of ASL, saying, ***"American Sign Language or ASL was developed many years ago to help people who could not hear or talk with each other. We are going to learn to use ASL as another way to remember the names of the letters in our alphabet."***
- ***"Let me show you the ASL chart."*** Place Transparency 4b on the overhead and point to the chart. ***"When we look at the chart, we can see that we have both lowercase letters and a picture of how you form your hand to make the 'sign' for that letter."*** Point to the letter/picture pair for the letter "a" on the chart as an example.
- ***"Let's try to make the letter 'a' with our hands."*** Show the students how to "sign" the letter "a" and check for understanding.
- Continue modeling using two more of the "signs" with the letters you have introduced thus far in your core reading program lessons.

*Guided Practice [Demonstrate]*

- ***"Now let's try those same letters again and see if you can remember how to make them with your hands."***

- Call out the same letters that you used to demonstrate earlier and see if the students can "sign" them.
- Offer support and guidance as needed.

*Independent Practice [Practice]*

Before independent work time, explain the activity to students and demonstrate how they will complete an accountability sheet.

1. Place the American Sign Language poster in your ABC center for students to practice making the hand signs during independent work time.
   - Place accountability sheets (black line of Transparency 4b) in the center for the students to record in the columns the letter pairs they found in their group of manipulatives.

2. Students will complete the activity sheet, Handout 4b, by pasting the letters in the left column and the American Sign Language picture matches in the right column.
   - Precut *five letter pairs* from the sheet provided and place them in plastic sandwich bags prior to the activity.

*Check for Understanding [Prove]*

- As the students are actively responding, you should provide corrective and/or supportive feedback.
- Note the students who are still having difficulty for extra practice during independent work time.

## Attachments

- Overhead transparency/black line master Transparency 4b.
- Cut and paste activity sheet Handout 4b.

| **Differentiation** | | |
|---|---|---|
| **Stage 1** | **Stage 2** | **Stage 3** |
| Follow the above procedures and gradually add letters as they are introduced in the core reading program. | Have pairs of students work together to read the chart and form the signs until they can sign the alphabet in order. | Have pairs of students sign words found around the room to each other. The person interpreting the signs must then locate the word in the room. |

# Transparency 4b

## American Sign Language Alphabet Match

| American Alphabet Letters | American Sign Language Hand Signs |
|---|---|
| | |
| | |
| | |
| | |
| | |

# Handout 4b

## American Sign Language Alphabet Match

Name: _____     Date: _____

Place the cut-out pictures of ASL hand signs on the table beside the sheet. Paste the hand sign pictures in the right column. Now, write the letter that matches the hand sign in the column to the left.

| Alphabet Letters | American Sign Language Hand Signs |
|---|---|
|  |  |
|  |  |
|  |  |
|  |  |
|  |  |

## Activity 4c: Distinguishing Uppercase and Lowercase Letters
## (Using Sense of Touch)

Purpose: The learner will [TLW] Identify letters using their sense of touch.

Sample Standard Course of Study [SCOS] Competency Goal Objective:

TLW recognize and name uppercase and lowercase letters of the alphabet (adapted from *Language Arts: Kindergarten*, n.d.).

### Grouping Strategies

| Whole Group | Small Group | Independent |
|---|---|---|
| Materials:<br><br>• Athletic sock with a cup placed inside<br>• Magnetic letters<br><br>*Optional:*<br><br>*Large chart to graph letters pulled*<br><br>*Crayons/markers* | Materials:<br><br>• Athletic sock with a cup placed inside<br>• Magnetic letters<br><br>*Optional:*<br><br>*Medium-size chart to graph letters pulled*<br><br>*Crayons/markers* | Materials:<br><br>• Athletic sock with a cup placed inside<br>• Magnetic letters<br>• Chart to graph letters pulled: HO4c<br>• Crayons/markers |

### Instructional Strategies [may be adapted as new letters are introduced in your reading program.]

*Input/Modeling [Demonstrate]*

- Explain to the student(s) the purpose of the activity: ***"Today we are going to use our sense of touch to identify some letters of the alphabet."***
- Show students the sock-covered cup and explain the purpose of the activity: ***"I have placed some magnetic letters in this sock. I am using only the letters we have learned so far in our reading lessons."*** Point to the sound/spelling cards above your board and your alphabet chart.
- ***"We are going play a special game today. I am going to let you slip your hand down in the sock and get a letter. You must pick up the first letter you touch. You must not take your hand out of the sock! As you touch the letter, I want you to determine the name of that letter. When you think you know the name of the letter, say the name out loud, and then pull your hand the rest of the way out so we can see if you are correct. If we think you are correct, we will touch our ear. If we do not think you are correct, we will touch our foot."***
- ***"Let me show you what I expect you to do."*** As you show them what you expect, review the procedures aloud. ***"If you think I am correct, touch your ear. If I am not correct, touch your foot. Good job!"***

- OPTIONAL: *"Now I am going to color in the box on my graph that is just above the letter I identified. I am going to color in this box since I pulled the letter _____."* Color in the correct box, modeling for the students what will be expected of them during independent work time.
- *"Remember, you cannot pull your letter out until you have told us the name of your letter."*

*Guided Practice [Demonstrate]*

- *"Now it's your turn to give it a try."*
- Call on several children to identify some of the letters using their sense of touch.
- OPTIONAL: Have the student color in the correct box on the class graph.
- Keep these materials ready for "filler" activities when you have a few minutes to spare.

*Independent Practice [Practice]*

Place the materials in your ABC center for students to practice identifying letters using their sense of touch during independent work time. (For accountability purposes, students will need to work with a partner so the partner can check an accuracy.)

- Students will complete the activity sheet, any one of Handouts 4c1–4c3, by coloring a block in the correct column on the graph each time they choose a letter.
- Write the letters contained in the sock/cup along the bottom of the graph. (The letters will depend on which ones you have introduced to them in class.)

*Check for Understanding [Prove]*

- As the students are actively responding, you should provide corrective and/or supportive feedback.
- Note the students who are still having difficulty for extra practice during independent work time.

**Attachment**

- Find the Letter Graph, any one of Handouts 4c1–4c3.

| **Differentiation** | | |
|---|---|---|
| **Stage 1** | **Stage 2** | **Stage 3** |
| Supply students with only two different letters they have learned in their lessons. The letters you use should not be visually/tactilely similar. Have multiple copies of the letters. *Example:* s, S, s, M, m, m | Supply students with no more than four different letters they have learned in their lessons. *Example:* S, s, M, m, A, a, p, P | Supply students with a variety of letters that they have been taught in their lessons. For best results, use no more than ten letters at a time as they perform the activity. |

# Handout 4c1

## Find the Letter Graph

Name: _____     Date: _____

Complete the graph below by coloring in a box in the correct column as you correctly identify the letters chosen from the sock/cup.

| | | | | My partner today was: |
|---|---|---|---|---|
| | | | | _____ |
| | | | | |
| | | | | Sum up the activity: |
| | | | | |
| | | | | |

# Handout 4c2

## Find the Letter Graph

Name: _____     Date: _____

Complete the graph below by coloring in a box in the correct column as you correctly identify the letters chosen from the sock/cup.

| | | | | | My partner today was: |
|---|---|---|---|---|---|
| | | | | | _____ |
| | | | | | Sum up the activity: |
| | | | | | |
| | | | | | |
| | | | | | |

# Handout 4c3

## Find the Letter Graph

Name: _____     Date: _____

Complete the graph below by coloring in a box in the correct column as you correctly identify the letters chosen from the sock/cup.

My partner today was:

_____

Sum up the activity:

# Activity 5: Distinguishing Letters/Sounds (Using Sense of Touch)

Purpose: The learner will [TLW] identify letter-sound relationships using sense of touch.

Sample Standard Course of Study [SCOS] Competency Goal Objective:

TLW recognize and name uppercase and lowercase letters of the alphabet (adapted from Language Arts: Kindergarten, n.d.).

## Grouping Strategies

| Whole Group | Small Group | Independent |
|---|---|---|
| Materials: | Materials: | Materials: |
| • Athletic sock with a cup placed inside | • Athletic sock with a cup placed inside | • Athletic sock with a cup placed inside |
| • Magnetic letters | • Magnetic letters | • Magnetic letters |
| • Picture cards | • Picture cards | • Chart to graph letters pulled: HO5 |
| | | • Crayons/markers |
| *Optional:* | *Optional:* | • Picture cards matching the magnetic letters you are using |
| *Large chart to graph letters pulled* | *Medium-size chart to graph letters pulled* | |
| *Crayons/markers* | *Crayons/markers* | |

## Instructional Strategies [may be adapted as new letters are introduced in your reading program.]

*Input/Modeling [Demonstrate]*

- Explain to the student(s) the purpose of the activity: ***"Today we are going to use our sense of touch to identify some letters of the alphabet."***
- Show students the sock-covered cup and explain the purpose of the activity: ***"I have placed some magnetic letters in a cup inside this sock. I am using only the letters we have learned so far in our reading lessons."*** Point to the sound/spelling cards above your board and your alphabet chart.
- ***"We are going to play a special game today. I am going to draw a sound/spelling card from this pile. Then I will let you slip your hand down in the sock and try to find the magnetic letter that matches the sound/spelling card. When you think you have found the letter, you must not take your hand out of the sock until I tell you to do so. When I tell you it is OK, pull your hand and the letter out so we can see if you are correct. If we think you are correct, we will touch our nose. If we do not think you are correct, we will touch our knee."***
- ***"Let me show you what I expect you to do."*** As you show them what you expect, review the procedures aloud. ***"If you think I am correct, touch your nose. If I am not correct, touch your knee. Good job!"***
- OPTIONAL: ***"Now I am going to color in the box on my graph that is just above the letter/sound I identified. I am going to color in this box since I pulled the letter/sound _____."*** Color in the correct

box, modeling for the students what will be expected of them during independent work time.

- ***"Remember, you cannot pull your letter out until I tell you to do so."***

*Guided Practice [Demonstrate]*

***"Now let's have one of you give it a try."***

- Call on several children to find the magnetic letter representing the first sound of the picture card or letter sound you prompt them to find.
- OPTIONAL: Have the student color in the correct box on the class graph.
- Keep the materials ready for impromptu or transition activities when you have a few minutes to spare.

*Independent Practice [Practice]*

Place the materials in your ABC center for students to practice identifying letters using their sense of touch during independent work time. (For accountability purposes, students will need to work with a partner so the partner can check for accuracy.) Write the letters contained in the sock/cup along the bottom of the graph. (The letters will depend on which ones you have introduced to them in class.)

- The student will draw a picture card from the pile provided.
- Then the student will put a hand inside the sock to find the letter that matches the first sound of the picture card.
- The partner will check whether the student is correct.
- If the student is correct, the students will complete the activity sheet, any one of Handouts 5a–5c, by coloring a block in the correct column on the graph each time they choose a letter.

*Check for Understanding [Prove]*

- As the students are actively responding, you should provide corrective and/or supportive feedback.
- Note the students who are still having difficulty for extra practice during independent work time.

## Attachment

- Find the Sound Graph, Handout 5 (a–d).

### Differentiation

| Stage 1 | Stage 2 | Stage 3 |
|---|---|---|
| Supply students with only two different letters they have learned in their lessons. The letters you use should not be visually/tactilely similar. Have multiple copies of the letters (e.g., s, S, s, M, m, m). | Supply students with no more than four different letters they have learned in their lessons (e.g., S, s, M, m, A, a, p, P). | Supply students with a variety of letters that they have been taught in their lessons. For best results, use no more than ten letters at a time as they perform the activity. |

# Handout 5a

## Find the Sound Graph

Name: _____     Date: _____

Complete the graph below by coloring in a box in the correct column as you correctly identify the letter/sounds chosen from the sock/cup.

| | |
|---|---|
| | |
| | |
| | |
| | |
| | |
| s | m |

My partner today was:

_____

Sum up the activity:

# Handout 5b

## Find the Sound Graph

Name: _____     Date: _____

Complete the graph below by coloring in a box in the correct column as you correctly identify the letter/sounds chosen from the sock/cup.

|  |  |  |
|---|---|---|
|  |  |  |
|  |  |  |
|  |  |  |
|  |  |  |
|  |  |  |

My partner today was:

_____

Sum up the activity:

# Handout 5c

## Find the Sound Graph

Name: _____     Date: _____

Complete the graph below by coloring in a box in the correct column as you correctly identify the letter/sounds chosen from the sock/cup.

| | | | | My partner today was: |
|---|---|---|---|---|
| | | | | _____ |
| | | | | Sum up the activity: |
| | | | | |

# Handout 5d

## Find the Sound Graph

Name: _____     Date: _____

Complete the graph below by coloring in a box in the correct column as you correctly identify the letter/sounds chosen from the sock/cup.

| | | | | | | My partner today was: |
|---|---|---|---|---|---|---|
| | | | | | | _____ |
| | | | | | | Sum up the activity: |
| | | | | | | |
| | | | | | | |
| | | | | | | |

# 3

# Initial Sound Fluency

*As intervention studies have shown over and over, children who do not grasp how the alphabet works are likely to need help developing phoneme awareness as well as knowledge of letter names and the sounds they represent. These are the most critical skills to teach in kindergarten if reading failure is to be prevented.*

Louisa Moats, *Speech to Print: Language Essentials for Teachers*, 2000

*S*trategies and Lessons for Improving Basic Early Literacy Skills Initial Sound Fluency Classroom Activities are stand-alone lessons. They can be used in any order with the exception of Silly Sentence and Letter/Sound Books, which are divided into two parts to keep the timing of the lesson to 15 minutes or less. These activities should be taught in order. The first part is for teaching, and the second part provides opportunities for guided practice. The other activities provide additional practice for initial sound fluency.

---

### Improving Initial Sound Fluency

Originally placed in second grade because of her age, Anna was soon moved to a first-grade classroom because she had no formal education before coming to the United States from Mexico. In addition, Anna's parents had very little formal schooling and spoke no English. She had not had any instruction with letters or sounds. Upon initial testing in September using the DIBELS assessments, a spelling inventory, and sight word checklist, Anna's teacher determined she would benefit from instruction using the activities for Initial Sound Fluency.

**Table 3.1**   Summary of Assessment for Anna in September

| **DIBELS Initial Sound Fluency** | **Sight Word Inventory Score** | **Spelling Inventory** |
|---|---|---|
| 0—Anna was unable to identify any initial sounds within the one minute assessment | 0—Anna was unable to read any of the sight words | Anna was unable to spell any words and identify any initial sounds of words |

As Anna's teacher introduced her to sounds/letters, she had her follow up the lesson with the Letter-Sound Book (Activity 8a/8b). Anna worked individually with her teacher throughout the year on this activity as well as with other Spanish-speaking students who could translate the directions for her. Anna was not only able to develop her knowledge of how letters and sounds work together through this activity but was also able to develop her English vocabulary skills. Her teacher noted that Anna's confidence grew significantly while working on her book. Anna began to participate more in class because she felt more knowledgeable about letters/sounds.

By the end of the school year, Anna was able to recognize all letters of the alphabet and use most sounds correctly while writing simple text. The graph below is a summary of Anna's progress using DIBELS progress monitoring and benchmark assessments on the initial sound fluency assessment; it shows consistent growth throughout the school year. Anna's teacher was able to use the scores from each month's assessment to plan further instruction for Anna and was able to help her meet benchmark level by the end of the school year.

**Figure 3.1**     Graph of Anna's Progress

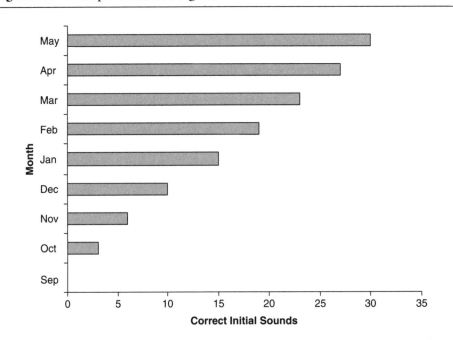

## Classroom Activities

Activity 6a: Silly Sentences—Part 1

Purpose: The learner will [TLW] create alliteration sentences using names of students in the classroom.

Sample Standard Course of Study [SCOS] Competency Goal Objective:

TLW demonstrate understanding of the sound of letters (adapted from *Language Arts: Kindergarten*, n.d.).

### Grouping Strategies

| Whole Group | Small Group | Independent |
|---|---|---|
| Materials:<br><br>• Chart paper or sentence strips<br>• Markers<br>• Chart stand or pocket chart<br><br>*Optional:*<br><br>*Overhead transparency*<br><br>*Overhead projector* | Materials:<br><br>• Chart tablet or sentence strips<br>• Big book stand or pocket chart<br>• Markers | Materials:<br><br>• Sentence strip<br>• Marker |

## Instructional Strategies

*Input/Modeling [Demonstrate]:*

- Explain the activity to the students: ***"Today we are going to begin creating 'silly sentences' using the names of the students in our class. Each day we will create a new silly sentence using a new name."***
- Display the chart tablet/sentence strip for all students to see. Model the activity by creating a silly sentence using your name.
- ***"Let's begin with my name. My name begins with an /m/ so I want most of my words to begin with the /m/ sound too."***
- Create an alliteration sentence and record your sentence on the strip. (Ex. Mrs. McClanahan makes marshmallow munchies.)
- Underline each /m/ sound at the beginning of each word and say to the students, ***"I am going to underline the /m/ sound as I read my sentence again."*** (Ex. Mrs. McClanahan makes marshmallow munchies.)

*Check for Understanding [Prove]:*

- Observe the students as you create your sentences.
- Call on different students to review the steps in the activity.

## Activity 6b: Silly Sentences—Part 2

Purpose: The learner will [TLW] create alliteration sentences using names of students in the classroom.

Sample Standard Course of Study [SCOS] Competency Goal Objective:

TLW demonstrate understanding of the sound of letters (adapted from *Language Arts: Kindergarten,* n.d.).

### Grouping Strategies

| Whole Group | Small Group | Independent |
|---|---|---|
| Materials:<br><br>• Chart paper or sentence strips<br>• Markers<br>• Chart stand or pocket chart<br><br>*Optional:*<br><br>*Overhead transparency*<br><br>*Overhead projector* | Materials:<br><br>• Chart tablet or sentence strips<br>• Big book stand or pocket chart<br>• Markers | Materials:<br><br>• Sentence strip<br>• Marker |

### Instructional Strategies

*Input/Modeling [Demonstrate]*

- Explain the activity to the students: ***"Today we are going to create a new silly sentence using the name of a student in our class."***
- Display the chart tablet/sentence strip for all students to see.
- Review the activity by rereading the silly sentence you and the class created in the previous lesson.

*Guided Practice [Demonstrate]*

Each day, create silly sentences using the procedures above for each student in the class.

- Ask students to help you come up with words that you might use to complete your silly sentence. ***"I would like your help creating our silly sentence today. We are going to create a new sentence with _____'s name. _____'s name begins with the /___/ sound. Does anyone know of another word that begins with the /___/ sound that we can use in our sentence?"***
- As students respond, make a list of their /___/ words.

- Once you have enough words to create a sentence say, ***"I think we have enough words to create a silly sentence for _____. Does anyone have any suggestions of a silly sentence for _____ using the words we came up with on our list?"***
- Record the silly sentence you and the class created on the chart tablet/sentence strip.
- As you reread the sentence, underline the initial /___/ sounds.
- For students with the same initial sounds in their names, you may want to combine the names into one sentence.

*Independent Practice [Practice]*

Option 1

1. In the writing center, have the students create their own silly sentences (dictated or written independently).

2. Students may illustrate their silly sentence.

Option 2

1. Create a class book of the silly sentences and place it in the book center. Each student may illustrate his or her page.

2. Keep the book in the book center for repeated readings.

Option 3

1. Show the students how you can illustrate your sentence by rereading the sentence and illustrating it to match the words in the silly sentence.

2. After creating a silly sentence for a particular student, have that student illustrate the sentence based on what was written on the sentence strip.

3. Place the sentence and illustration in the book center for others to read.

*Check for Understanding [Prove]*

- Observe the students as you create your sentences.
- Call on different students to respond and make a note of the students who cannot respond appropriately to the task for pullout groups during independent work time.

## Differentiation

| Stage 1 | Stage 2 | Stage 3 |
|---|---|---|
| Use the names of the students that begin with the "stop" sounds. (/t/, /k/, /b/, /d/, /g/, etc.) | Use the names of the students that begin with the "continuous" sounds. (/f/, /h/, /m/, /n/, /z/, etc.) | Use the names of the students that begin with vowel sounds. |

# Activity 7: Picture/Sound Charts

Purpose: The learner will [TLW] create charts with the teacher to represent the letter/sound introduced in the lesson.

Sample Standard Course of Study [SCOS] Competency Goal Objective:

TLW demonstrate understanding of the sound of letters (adapted from *Language Arts: Kindergarten*, n.d.).

## Grouping Strategies

| Whole Group | Small Group | Independent |
|---|---|---|
| Materials: <br><br> • Large construction paper cut in half the long way <br> • Markers <br> • Chart stand or another way to display the blank strips of construction paper <br><br> *Optional:* <br><br> *Overhead transparency* <br> *Overhead projector* | Materials: <br><br> • Large construction paper cut in half the long way <br> • Markers <br> • Chart stand or another way to display the blank strips of construction paper | Materials: <br><br> • Small construction paper cut in half the long way <br> • Markers |

## Instructional Strategies

*Input/Modeling [Demonstrate]*

- Explain the activity to the students: ***"Today we are going to begin creating lists of pictures/words to represent the letters we learn in our reading lessons."***
- Display the construction paper for all students to see.
- ***"First, we need to write the letter ___ at the top of our paper."***
- ***"Now, let me think of some words that begin with that sound."*** Think aloud for two to three examples.
- ***"First, I will draw my picture of __ball__ since I know it begins with the __/b/__ sound. Then, just under that picture, I will draw a __boy__ and then I will draw my final picture under my second."***
- ***"If you know how to write the word for the picture, you can do that too."***

*Guided Practice [Demonstrate]*

- ***"Now, I would like your help thinking of words and pictures we can add to our letter/sound chart."***

- As students respond, make a list of their __/b/__ pictures/words.
- Once you have enough words, say, ***"I think we have enough words on our chart for today. Let's go back over our chart together to say the words/pictures we created for the letter __b__ ."***
- As you reread the words, if you chose to write them, underline the initial sounds.
- Post the chart in the room for reference during future sound to letter lessons.

*Independent Practice [Practice]*

Option 1

1. In the writing center, have the students create their own letter/sound chart. (dictated or written independently)

Option 2

1. Create a class book of the letter/sound charts for the book center. Each student may illustrate his or her page.

2. Keep the book in the book center for repeated readings.

*Check for Understanding [Prove]*

- Observe the students as you create the class charts.
- Call on different students to respond/clarify their suggestions and make a note of the students who cannot respond appropriately to the task for pullout groups during independent work time.

| Differentiation: (If you do not follow core reading program lesson plans) | | |
|---|---|---|
| **Stage 1** | **Stage 2** | **Stage 3** |
| Use the letters that begin with the "stop" sounds. (/t/, /k/, /b/, /d/, /g/, etc.) | Use the letters that begin with the "continuous" sounds. (/f/, /h/, /m/, /n/, /z/, etc.) | Use the names of the students that begin with vowel sounds. |

## Activity 8a: Letter/Sound Books—Part 1

Purpose: The learner will [TLW] create letter/sound books as letter/sounds are introduced in the core reading program.

Sample Standard Course of Study [SCOS] Competency Goal Objective:

TLW demonstrate understanding of the sound of letters (adapted from *Language Arts: Kindergarten*, n.d.).

## Grouping Strategies

| Whole Group | Small Group | Independent |
|---|---|---|
| Materials:<br><br>• Chart tablet (to model creating pages in a book)<br>• Markers<br>• Chart stand<br>• Various ABC books on display<br><br>*Optional:*<br><br>*Blank overhead transparencies*<br><br>*Overhead projector*<br><br>*Letter/sound charts created in Activity 7 on display in the room* | Materials:<br><br>• Small chart tablet (to model creating pages in a book)<br>• Big book stand or pocket chart<br>• Blank student ABC book<br>• Markers/crayons/colored pencils<br>• Various ABC books on display<br><br>*Optional:*<br><br>*Letter/sound charts created in Activity 7 on display in the room*<br><br>*Separate sheets of blank paper*<br><br>*(Choose the best pages from those created to create a class book to place in the book center.)* | Materials:<br><br>• Blank student ABC book<br>• Markers/crayons/colored pencils<br>• Various ABC books on display<br><br>*Optional:*<br><br>*Keep student sheets separate and create a "class" book when all pages are complete.*<br><br>*Letter/sound charts created in Activity 7 on display in the room* |

## Instructional Strategies

This activity is the introduction to Activity 8b. It should be taught for several days in a row.

*Input/Modeling [Demonstrate]*

- Explain the activity to the students: ***"Today we are going to begin creating a class letter/sound book. As we work on our class book, you will have an opportunity to create your own letter/sound book during independent work time in the ABC center."***
- Point to the ABC books you have on display and talk about how the authors created the different books, but all have pictures that represent the letter/sounds for each letter of the alphabet.
- ***"Today we are going to make one page in our ABC book. Since we have talked about the letter _____ in our lesson, we are going to begin with that letter."***
- Turn to the page that will have that letter on it. For example, if the letter is "s," go through the book until you get to the page that should have the letter "s" written on it.
- ***"Since this is our first page, I am going to create the first page in our book and show you how I think when I create a page in an ABC book."***

- *"First I need to write the letter ___ on my page. I think I will write my letter up here at the top of my page. I like the books that have both the uppercase letter and the lowercase letter, so I am going to use both of them in our class book. Remember, if you forget how to make the letter, you can always check our alphabet picture cards or the ABC chart in our ABC center."*
- *"Now I need to think of how I want to illustrate my page with words that begin with /___/. I know I can think of my own pictures/words or I can 'read the room' to come up with ideas to illustrate my page. One place in particular I know that I can look is our letter/sound charts we made in class."* (Refer to Activity 7b.) Say the sound of the letter several times and brainstorm out loud different words that begin with that sound.
- Continue to think aloud as you illustrate your letter/sound page.

### Check for Understanding [Prove]

- Observe the students as you create your ABC book.
- Call on different students to respond and make a note of the students who cannot respond appropriately to the task for pullout groups during independent work time.

## Activity 8b: Letter/Sound Books—Part 2

Purpose: The learner will [TLW] create letter/sound books as they are introduced in the core reading program.

Sample Standard Course of Study [SCOS] Competency Goal Objective:

TLW demonstrate understanding of the sound of letters (adapted from *Language Arts: Kindergarten*, n.d.).

## Instructional Strategies

Once Activity 8a is established, this lesson, Activity 8b, should be taught for several days in a row until the task is established.

### Input/Modeling [Demonstrate]

- Explain the activity to the students: *"Today we are going to work on your letter/sound book. Before we begin on your book, let's look at the books on display and our class book to review how we create a page in an ABC book."*
- Point to the ABC books you have on display and talk about how the authors created the different books and that all have pictures that represent the letter/sounds for each letter of the alphabet.
- Quickly review how the class page was created the day before.

## Grouping Strategies

| Whole Group | Small Group | Independent |
|---|---|---|
| Materials:<br><br>• Chart tablet (to model creating pages in a book)<br>• Markers<br>• Chart stand<br>• Various ABC books on display<br><br>*Optional:*<br><br>*Blank overhead transparencies*<br><br>*Overhead projector* | Materials:<br><br>• Small chart tablet (to model creating pages in a book)<br>• Big book stand or pocket chart<br>• Blank student ABC book<br>• Markers/crayons/colored pencils<br>• Various ABC books on display<br><br>*Optional:*<br><br>*Separate sheets of blank paper*<br><br>*(Choose the best pages from those created to create a class book to place in the book center.)* | Materials:<br><br>• Blank student ABC book<br>• Markers/crayons/colored pencils<br>• Various ABC books on display<br><br>*Optional:*<br><br>*Keep student sheets separate and create a "class" book when all pages are complete.* |

- ***"Today we are going to make one page in your ABC book. Since we have talked about the letter ___ in our reading lesson, we are going to begin with that letter."***
- Pass out the individual ABC books and turn the pages together with the students until you get to the page for the letter you are working on today.

*Guided Practice [Demonstrate]*

- ***"First you need to write the letter ___ on your page. Think where you want to write your letter and if you want to write both the uppercase and lowercase, or just one of them. Remember, if you forget how to make the letter, you can always check our alphabet picture cards or the ABC chart in our ABC center or any of our displays in our room to help you."***
- Once all the students have written their letters, say: ***"Now you need to think of how you want to illustrate your page with pictures/words that begin with /___/. Where are some places in our room that you can refer to that will help you think of a picture that you can draw on your page?"*** Encourage them to use the sound/spelling cards and the charts the class created in Activity 7.

*Independent Practice [Practice]*

1. Place the individual books in the ABC center for the students to continue to work on during independent work time.

*Check for Understanding [Prove]*

- Observe the students as they create their ABC books and support as needed.

# Activity 9: Sound Collages

Purpose: The learner will [TLW] create sound collages as sounds are introduced in the core reading program.

Sample Standard Course of Study [SCOS] Competency Goal Objective:

TLW demonstrate understanding of the sound of letters (adapted from *Language Arts: Kindergarten*, n.d.).

## Grouping Strategies

| Whole Group | Small Group | Independent |
|---|---|---|
| Materials:<br><br>• Chart tablet (to model creating pages in a book)<br>• Large size construction paper<br>• Markers<br>• Chart stand<br>• Glue<br>• Old magazines<br>• Examples of collages: "I Spy" books<br><br>*Optional:*<br><br>*Chart tablet (to model creating pages in a book)* | Materials:<br><br>• Small chart tablet (to model creating pages in a book)<br>• Big book stand or pocket chart<br>• Small size construction paper or blank student ABC collage books<br>• Markers/crayons/colored pencils<br>• Glue<br>• Old magazines<br>• Examples of collages: "I Spy" books<br><br>*Optional:*<br><br>*Separate sheets of blank paper*<br><br>*(Choose the best pages from those created to make a class book to place in the book center.)* | Materials:<br><br>• Blank student ABC collage books<br>• Markers/crayons/colored pencils<br>• Examples of collages: "I Spy" books<br><br>*Optional:*<br><br>*Keep student sheets separate and create a "class" book when all pages are complete.* |

## Instructional Strategies

*Input/Modeling [Demonstrate]*

- Explain the activity to the students: ***"Today we are going to work in groups to make 'sound collages.' After we create our collages, we are going to display them in our room so we can refer to them as we need to during our day."***

- *"Does anyone know what a collage is?"*
- *"Super! A collage is a group of pictures put very close together. I have some books with examples of collages."* Show examples and discuss how collages are created.
- *"Let me demonstrate what I want you to do with your group. First, each group will have a different letter. I am going to make a collage of the letter ___."* Use only letters that have been introduced previously in your core reading program lessons.
- *"I am going to look through my magazine and try to find a picture that begins with the letter _____. Ahh! Here is one. _____ (name of picture) begins with the _____ sound and I know that sound is for the letter _____. Now I am going to cut it out, put glue on the back, and place it on my page. Then I am going to find other pictures that begin with the letter _____, which makes the sound _____."*
- Explain to the students that they need to continue until their page is completely filled with pictures that begin with the letter/sound you assigned.

*Guided Practice [Demonstrate]*

- *"I am going to give each group an assigned letter, a large piece of construction paper, glue, scissors, and some old magazines. I don't want you to tell the other groups your letter. I want to see if they can guess what letter you had when they look at your collage."*

*Independent Practice [Practice]*

Place the individual books in the ABC center for the students to continue to work on their own personal ABC collage book during independent work time.

*Check for Understanding [Prove]*

- Observe the students as they create their collages. Support as needed throughout the activity.
- Hold up one of the posters the groups made and have the others guess what their letter was. Call on volunteers who raise their hands.

### Differentiation

| Stage 1 | Stage 2 | Stage 3 |
|---------|---------|---------|
| Students may work in groups to complete the activity. | Students may work with a partner to complete the activity. | A student may complete the activity independently. |

# Activity 10: Sound Identification Game

Purpose: The learner will [TLW] confirm or discount sound to letter matches.

Sample Standard Course of Study [SCOS] Competency Goal Objective:

TLW demonstrate understanding of the sound of letters (adapted from *Language Arts: Kindergarten,* n.d.).

## Grouping Strategies

| Whole Group | Small Group | Independent |
|---|---|---|
| Materials:<br><br>• Pocket chart<br>• Pictures representing sounds students have learned previously<br><br>*Optional:*<br><br>*Overhead transparencies of pictures* | Materials:<br><br>• Pocket chart<br>• Pictures representing sounds students have learned previously<br>• Individual picture card set for each student<br><br>*Optional:*<br><br>*Overhead transparencies of pictures* | Materials:<br><br>• Individual picture cards<br>• Accountability sheet |

## Instructional Strategies

*Input/Modeling [Demonstrate]*

- Explain the activity to the students: ***"Today we are going to do a quick review of some of the 'sounds' we have learned so far this year in our reading lessons, and I need your help."***
- Display the pocket chart with the row of pictures representing the sounds to review.
- ***"I have a row of pictures here on my chart. They are map, puzzle, apple, star. I am going to ask you to find and then show me the picture that begins with a particular sound."***
- ***"Let me show you what I mean. Find the picture that begins with /s/."*** You should go through each picture and 'think aloud' your decision-making process until you make your choice of "star." Hold the picture of the star toward your chest.
- ***"Now, don't let anyone see your card until I say, 'Show me.' OK. Show me."*** Turn the card around and show the students.
- Do as many examples as needed to make sure the students understand the task.

- *"I am going to give you a baggie with the pictures so you can play the game with me. Everyone take out your cards and place them in front of you."*
- *"Now, remember, do not show anyone the card you chose. Make sure you hide it against your chest. Here we go."*
- *"Find the picture that begins with /s/."* Give all students time to find their card and "hide" it against their chest.
- *"Show me."* Check students' responses for accuracy and allow students to correct themselves.
- *"Great job! Let's try some more."* Call out the other sounds for the pictures you have and follow the same procedures as outlined above.

*Independent Practice [Practice]*

1. Pass out the handout and explain the activity to the students.

2. They are to circle all of the /m/'s on the page.

*Check for Understanding [Prove]*

- Observe the students as you go through the activity.
- Call on several students to respond independently.
- Check the independent practice handout and reteach during independent work time as needed.

| Differentiation | | |
|---|---|---|
| **Stage 1** | **Stage 2** | **Stage 3** |
| Use only two different letter sounds represented on the cards/transparency. | Use three different letter sounds on the cards/transparency. | Use four letter sounds represented on the cards/transparency. |

**Attachments:**

- Overhead Transparency/Initial Sound Fluency Picture Cards Transparency 10
- Overhead Transparency/Initial Sound Fluency Handout 10

# Handout 10

## Initial Sound Fluency Picture Cards

# Transparency 10

# Activity 11: Picture/Sound Identification Game

Purpose: The learner will [TLW] confirm or discount sound to letter matches.

Sample Standard Course of Study [SCOS] Competency Goal Objective:

TLW demonstrate understanding of the sound of letters (adapted from *Language Arts: Kindergarten, n.d.*).

## Grouping Strategies

| Whole Group | Small Group | Independent |
|---|---|---|
| Materials:<br><br>• Pocket chart<br>• Pictures cards<br>• Pocket chart stand<br><br>*Optional:*<br><br>*Overhead transparency of picture cards*<br><br>*DIBELS Progress Monitoring Pictures from previous assessments* | Materials:<br><br>• Pocket chart<br>• Picture cards<br>• Pocket chart stand<br><br>*Optional:*<br><br>*Overhead transparency of picture cards*<br><br>*DIBELS Progress Monitoring Pictures from previous assessments* | Materials:<br><br>• Picture cards<br>• Accountability sheet<br><br>*Optional:*<br><br>*DIBELS Progress Monitoring Pictures from previous assessments* |

## Instructional Strategies

*Input/Modeling [Demonstrate]*

- Explain the activity to the students: ***"Today we are going to do a quick review of some of the sounds we have learned so far this year in our reading lessons, and I need your help."***
- Display the pocket chart with four picture cards representing the sounds the children have learned so far this year.
- ***"I have picture cards here in our pocket chart. This is man, sun, soap, money. (Point to each picture and say its name.) I am going to point to one card at a time and ask you a question. You will need to answer either 'yes' or 'no' as I snap my fingers."***
- ***"Let me show you what I mean."*** Point to the first picture on the chart and ask, ***"Does this begin with an /m/?"*** Snap your fingers and say, ***"Yes. Does this begin with an /m/?"*** Snap your fingers and say, ***"No. Does this begin with an /m/?"*** Snap your fingers and say, ***"No. Does this begin with an /m/?"*** Snap your fingers and say, ***"Yes."***

*Guided Practice [Demonstrate]*

- *"Now you try it with me."* Point to the first picture on the chart again, ask the question, and snap your fingers until everyone understands the task.
- *"Great job! Let's try some more."* Point to the rest of the pictures in the row and ask the same question, *"Does this begin with an /m/?"* Snap *your fingers* and wait for their response. Praise/correct students as needed.
- *"Now, I am going to go over the names of our pictures again and ask you another question. This is man, sun, soap, money."* Point to one picture at a time and ask, *"Does this begin with /s/?"*

*Independent Practice [Practice]*

1. Pass out the handout and explain the activity to the students.

2. They are to circle all of the pictures that begin with /m/ on the page.

3. They are to cross out all of the pictures that begin with /s/ on the page.

*Check for Understanding [Prove]*

- Observe the students as you go through the activity.
- Call on several students to respond independently.
- Check the independent practice handout and reteach during independent work time as needed.

## Differentiation

| Stage 1 | Stage 2 | Stage 3 |
|---|---|---|
| Use only two different sound pictures on the cards/chart/transparency/handouts. | Use three different sound pictures on the cards/chart/transparency/handouts. | Use four different sound pictures on the cards/chart/transparency/handouts. |

## Attachments

- Overhead Transparency/Initial Sound Fluency Picture Cards Transparency 11
- Accountability Sheet/Initial Sound Fluency Handout 10

# Transparency 11

## Initial Sound Fluency Picture Cards

# Handout 11

## Identifying Initial Sounds

Name: _____    Date: _____

Circle all of the pictures that begin with the sound /m/. Cross out all the pictures that begin with the sound /s/.

# 4

# Phoneme Segmentation Fluency

*Teaching sounds along with the letters of the alphabet is important because it helps children to see how phonemic awareness relates to their reading and writing. Learning to blend phonemes with letters helps children read words. Learning to segment sounds with letters helps them spell words.*

National Institute for Literacy (2003)

The *Strategies and Lessons for Improving Basic Early Literacy Skills* Phoneme Segmentation Fluency Classroom Activities are designed to be taught in sequential order. Activity 12 prepares the students for isolating the sounds within words by teaching them to elongate the sounds in the words. Once the majority of your students have mastered Activity 12, you are then ready to move to Activity 13. Activity 13 moves on to the next step of identifying the number of sounds heard within a word. It may take several days or weeks for the students to master this concept. Once the majority of students have mastered Activity 13, you are ready to move from counting the sounds to creating a strategy for identifying the sequence of sounds through the use of Elkonin boxes.

Elkonin boxes are an instructional method used in the early elementary grades to build phonological awareness by segmenting words into syllables or sounds. They are named after D. B. Elkonin, the Russian psychologist who pioneered their use. The "boxes" are squares drawn on a piece of paper or a chalkboard, with one box for each syllable or phoneme, depending on what kind of segmentation is being done. To use Elkonin boxes, a child listens to a word and moves a token into a box for each syllable or phoneme. In some cases, different colored tokens may be used for consonants and vowels or just for each phoneme in the word. The purpose of Elkonin boxes is to help the child think about the order of sounds in spoken words. There are six steps developed by Elkonin and adapted by Clay to scaffold students as they learn to hear and record the sounds in words in sequence. They are: (1) Stretching Words/Slow Articulation, (2) Establishing the Task of Sound Boxes, (3) Sound Boxes, (4) Transition Boxes, (5) Letter Boxes, and (6) Independent Writing without use of boxes. The teacher's role throughout the activities is to model and provide guided practice until the students master the strategies of hearing sounds in words in sequential order. Although using Elkonin boxes may not strictly involve "phonemic awareness," we have included them in this section (Activities 13a–13e) because they focus attention on the manipulation of letters and sounds.

### Improving Phoneme Segmentation Fluency

All of the students in Mrs. Miller's first-grade class were performing at the entry level for kindergarten. These 18 students were identified across the grade level and intentionally placed in one classroom to give the teacher the opportunity to help these students make two years' growth in one year. The students all lived below the poverty level, 70% were Limited English Proficient, and all had been enrolled in an American school for at least one year.

In the beginning of the school year, Mrs. Miller and the literacy teacher administered the DIBELS assessments. All 18 students scored at a 5 or less on their Phoneme Segmentation Fluency Assessment. Since benchmark was 35 for that time of year, the teachers knew immediate intervention was needed to establish phonemic awareness skills.

The teachers divided the students into small groups and began working with them daily to establish phonemic awareness skills. The teachers began by demonstrating how to "stretch" sounds in words by using a rubber band (Activity 12). Once students were able to "stretch" one and two syllable words, the teachers began using the Elkonin boxes Activities in small groups. They first used Activity 13 and taught students to segment sounds and count the number of sounds they had said using three-sound words. Once students had mastered that skill, the teacher taught them to push the sounds with more complex words that had four or more sounds. When the students were able to segment and count the sounds in a word, the teachers worked with them to write the sounds they heard (Activity 13e). By writing the sounds down, the students became much more confident during Writer's Workshop because they were able to pull apart the sounds in the words they wanted to write, and they were also able to read their own writing. The confidence of all 18 children grew not only during the small-group sessions where they were segmenting sounds but also during Writer's Workshop.

The teacher used progress monitoring throughout the beginning of the year and saw consistent growth with all 18 students each week in the area of phoneme segmentation fluency. During the midyear benchmark in January, 16 of the 18 students were identified as no longer being at risk in the area of phoneme segmentation fluency. Table 4.1 illustrates each student's growth from beginning of the year to midyear.

Both Mrs. Miller and the literacy teacher believed that the small-group focused activities designed to address student skill needs helped each child make large gains in the area of phonemic awareness and phoneme segmentation ability.

**Table 4.1**   Mrs. Miller's First Grade (Benchmark Assessments)

| Student | September PSF | January PSF |
|---------|:---:|:---:|
| Andrea | 2 | 39 |
| Angela | 0 | 38 |
| Daniel | 4 | 45 |
| Danielle | 2 | 38 |
| David | 2 | 37 |
| Eduardo | 0 | 32 |
| Ian | 3 | 47 |
| John | 4 | 40 |
| Jose | 0 | 43 |
| Juan | 2 | 38 |
| Julia | 0 | 39 |
| Lucero | 4 | 44 |
| Manuel | 3 | 43 |
| Marco | 5 | 45 |
| Maria | 2 | 44 |
| Martin | 4 | 45 |
| Paco | 0 | 30 |
| Sara | 3 | 52 |

# Classroom Activities

## Activity 12: "Stretching" Sounds in Words

Purpose: The learner will [TLW] "stretch" words using a prop (e.g., rubber band) as a tactile device to model the strategy of slowly articulating a word in order to hear all the sounds within a word.

Sample Standard Course of Study [SCOS] Competency Goal Objectives.

TLW demonstrate that spoken language is a sequence of identifiable speech sounds (adapted from *Language Arts: Kindergarten*, n.d.).

TLW segment the phonemes of one syllable words (adapted from *Language Arts: First Grade*, n.d.).

## Grouping Strategies

| Whole Group | Small Group | Independent |
|---|---|---|
| Materials: <br><br>• Large rubber bands or thick piece of elastic <br><br>*Optional:* <br><br>*Pictures for overhead representing the words you are stretching* <br><br>*Overhead projector* | Materials: <br><br>• "Thick" rubber bands or "skinny" balloons <br><br>*Optional:* <br><br>*Picture cards representing the words you are stretching* <br><br>*Pocket chart to display picture cards* | Materials: <br><br>• "Thick" rubber bands <br><br>*Optional:* <br><br>*Picture cards representing the words you are stretching* |

## Instructional Strategies

*Input/Modeling [Demonstrate]*

- Explain to the student(s) the purpose of the activity: ***"We're going to practice saying a word slowly—stretching the word so that we can hear all of the sounds in the word."***
- Model the strategy for the students by "stretching" the elastic/rubber band while you slowly articulate the word "cat": /c . . . a . . . t . . . /.

*Guided Practice [Demonstrate]*

- ***"Let's try this together."*** Instruct the students to say the word "cat" slowly with you as you "stretch" the band.
- Give each student his or her own prop to "stretch" and together "stretch" the word "cat."
- Display the picture of the word "he" and follow the two procedures above.
- Continue to stretch the picture cards/words: pig, mom, mat, cap, stop, bee, tree. (Make sure you select words in which each sound is clearly heard—avoid r- and l-controlled vowels.)

*Independent Practice [Practice]*

Place rubber bands and picture cards of some common objects in a center for students to practice during independent work time.

*Check for Understanding [Prove]*

- Allow some/all students to demonstrate their "stretching" technique independently.

## Attachments

- See following pages for pictures to place on cards.

## Differentiation

| Stage 1 | Stage 2 | Stage 3 |
| --- | --- | --- |
| "Stretch" the words using a prop as a tactile device to emulate the process of slowly articulating a word in order to hear all the sounds within *one syllable words*. | "Stretch" the words with an *imaginary* rubber band in your hands. Begin to use some words with *two syllables*. (e.g., hammer, circus, mother, father) | "Stretch" the words *without* using a prop. Begin using words with *two or more syllables*. (e.g., telephone, elephant, family) |

# Pictures for Cards

## Activity 13a: Elkonin Boxes—Identifying Sounds With Fingers

Prerequisite: Elongate sounds within a word, Activity 12

Purpose: TLW hear all sounds in spoken words, isolate those sounds, and think about the order of those sounds.

Sample Standard Course of Study [SCOS] Competency Goal Objectives:

TLW demonstrate that spoken language is a sequence of identifiable speech sounds (adapted from *Language Arts: Kindergarten,* n.d.).

TLW segment the phonemes of one syllable words (adapted from *Language Arts: First Grade,* n.d.).

### Instructional Strategies

This activity should be taught for several days in a row using other examples.

*Input/Modeling [Demonstrate]*

- Explain to the student(s) the purpose of the activity: ***"Now that you know how to stretch words, we are going to listen to see if we can hear how many sounds we hear in each word we stretch."***
- Show a picture of a cat and say, ***"I have a picture of a cat. I am going to stretch the word 'cat' so that I can hear all the sounds in the word: /cccaaattt/."***
- ***"Now I am going to use my fingers to help me figure out how many sounds I hear in the word 'cat.'"*** This time as you slowly articulate, hold up one finger at a time as you isolate the sounds. (Make sure your fingers are facing the children so they see them go up from left to right.)
- ***"I have three fingers up, so I know that I hear three sounds in the word 'cat.'"***

### Grouping Strategies

| Whole Group | Small Group | Independent |
|---|---|---|
| Materials:<br><br>• Picture cards<br>• Pocket chart to display picture cards<br><br>*Optional:*<br><br>*Pictures for overhead representing the words you are stretching*<br><br>*Overhead projector* | Materials:<br><br>• Markers<br>• Picture cards<br>• Pocket chart to display picture cards<br><br>*Optional:*<br><br>*Picture cards representing the words you are stretching*<br><br>*Pocket chart to display picture cards* | Materials:<br><br>• "Thick" rubber bands<br><br>*Optional:*<br><br>*Picture cards representing the words you are stretching* |

*Guided Practice [Demonstrate]*

- *"Now, let's try it together. Everybody stretch the word cat with me. Get your 'pretend' rubber bands ready. OK, here we go: /cccaaattt/."*
- *"Good, now let's try to use our fingers to help us count how many sounds we hear in the word 'cat.' Get your fingers up, get ready, let's go . . . /cccaaattt/."*
- *"Super!"*

*Check for Understanding [Prove]*

- *"Let's try another word. Here is a picture of a dog. First, let's stretch the word together—/dddoooggg/. Now, let's use our fingers to count how many sounds are in the word 'dog': /dddoooggg/."* Look around and check, then call on a child who has the correct number of fingers up to tell the class how many sounds were in the word "dog."
- Observe the students who are still having difficulty for pullout groups during independent work time.

| **Differentiation** | | |
|---|---|---|
| **Stage 1** | **Stage 2** | **Stage 3** |
| Practice with words that have two distinct sounds. *Example:* go, he, me, it, is . . . | Practice with words that have three to four distinct sounds. *Example:* man, sun, tree, house . . . | Practice with words that have more than four sounds. *Example:* start, puppy, friend . . . |

## Activity 13b: Elkonin Boxes—Pushing Sounds

Prerequisite: Elongate sounds within a word, Activity 12

Purpose: TLW hear all sounds in spoken words, isolate those sounds, and think about the order of those sounds.

Sample Standard Course of Study [SCOS] Competency Goal Objectives:

TLW demonstrate that spoken language is a sequence of identifiable speech sounds (adapted from *Language Arts: Kindergarten,* n.d.).

TLW segment the phonemes of one syllable words (adapted from *Language Arts: First Grade,* n.d.).

### Grouping Strategies

| Whole Group | Small Group | Independent |
|---|---|---|
| Materials:<br><br>• Large rubber bands or thick pieces of elastic<br>• Chart paper or board to pre-write Elkonin boxes<br>• Markers<br>• Picture cards<br>• Pocket chart to display picture cards<br>• If your board is magnetic, use round magnets as "markers/chips" as you push the sound into boxes.<br><br>*Optional:*<br><br>*Elkonin boxes on overhead transparencies*<br><br>*Pictures for overhead representing the words you are stretching*<br><br>*Overhead projector* | Materials:<br><br>• "Thick" rubber bands or "skinny" balloons<br>• Chart paper or board to pre-write Elkonin boxes<br>• Index cards with Elkonin boxes<br>• Markers<br>• Picture cards<br>• Pocket chart to display picture cards<br>• "Markers/chips"* for manipulating while pushing sounds into boxes<br><br>*Optional:*<br><br>*Picture cards representing the words you are stretching*<br><br>*Pocket chart to display picture cards* | Materials:<br><br>• "Thick" rubber bands<br>• Index cards with Elkonin boxes<br>• "Markers/chips"* for manipulating while pushing sounds into boxes.<br><br>*Optional:*<br><br>*Picture cards representing the words you are stretching*<br><br>* *"markers/chips" may be game chips, milk carton tops, two-liter bottle tops, checkers, etc.* |

### Instructional Strategies

This activity should be taught for several days in a row using different examples.

*Input/Modeling [Demonstrate]*

- Explain to the student(s) the purpose of the activity: **"Now that you know how to hear how many sounds we hear in each word we** *stretch, we are going to learn how to push the sounds we hear into 'boxes.'"*

- Show a picture of a cat and say: *"I have a picture of a cat. I am going to stretch the word 'cat' so that I can hear all the sounds in the word: /cccaaattt/."*
- *"Now I am going to use my fingers to help me figure out how many sounds I hear in the word 'cat.'"* This time as you slowly articulate, hold up one finger at a time as you isolate the sounds. (Make sure your fingers are facing the children so they see them go up from left to right.)
- *"I have three fingers up, so I know that I hear three sounds in the word 'cat.'"*
- *"I am going to draw three boxes up here on our chart/board."* Draw three connecting boxes on the board and place a magnetic marker under each box. *"I am going to put these three magnets here under each box. As I say the word 'cat' I am going to push the magnets up into the boxes as I say each sound slowly."*
- Demonstrate how to "push" the sound in the boxes as you slowly articulate the word "cat."

### Guided Practice [Demonstrate]

- *"Now, let's try it together. Everybody stretch the word cat with me. Get your pretend rubber bands ready. OK, here we go, /cccaaattt/."*
- *"Good, now let's try to use our fingers to help us count how many sounds we hear in the word 'cat.' Get your fingers up, get ready, let's go . . . /cccaaattt/."*
- *"Super!"*
- *"Now, we already have our three boxes, so as we say the word slowly, I would like _____ to come up here to show us how to push the sounds into the boxes."* Make sure the first child you call on is one who will be successful. Then call on several other children to try pushing the sounds in the boxes as the rest of the class slowly articulates the word, "cat."

### Independent Practice [Practice]

When the children are in control of the task and beginning to record all of the sounds in sequence, you are ready to move to using letter boxes during their independent writing. Use one side of their journal as their "practice page." This will be the page on which they can draw their boxes and record the sounds they hear to support their journal writing.

### Check for Understanding [Prove]

- *"Let's try another word. Here is a picture of a dog. First, let's stretch the word together: /dddoooggg/. Now, let's use our fingers to count how many sounds are in the word 'dog': /dddoooggg/."* Look around to check, then call on a child who has the correct number of fingers up to tell the class how many sounds were in the word "dog."

- *"Everybody, show me on your fingers how many boxes I need to draw on our board. Fantastic! You all are so smart! Yes, I do need three boxes."*
- Go back to the board where you have the three boxes and count the number of boxes with the students to confirm that you have three boxes already on the board.
- *"Now, everybody slowly articulate the word 'dog' with me and pretend to push the sounds into the boxes as I push the sounds into the boxes up here."*
- Do it several times and watch the children to make sure they are "pushing" the sounds into their imaginary boxes.
- Note the students who are having difficulty for pullout groups during independent work time.

### Differentiation

| Stage 1 | Stage 2 | Stage 3 |
|---|---|---|
| Words/pictures with two boxes | Words/pictures with three boxes | Words/pictures with four or more boxes |

## Attachments

- Overhead Transparency/Elkonin Sound Boxes Transparency 13b1–13b3 and copies of them to paste on index cards
- Phoneme Lists Handout 13b

# Transparency 13b1

## Elkonin Boxes—Sound Boxes

| | |
|---|---|
| | |

# Transparency 13b2

## Elkonin Boxes—Transition Boxes

| | | |
|---|---|---|
| | | |

# Transparency 13b3

## Elkonin Boxes—Pushing Boxes

| | | | |
|---|---|---|---|
| | | | |

# Handout 13b

## Phoneme Lists

EXAMPLES:

Add to this list as you come across words to include in the categories.

| Two Phoneme Words | Three Phoneme Words | Three or More Phoneme Words With Blends and Digraphs |
|---|---|---|
| bee   **YOUR WORDS** | bat   **YOUR WORDS** | bail   **YOUR WORDS** |
| bow | cat | bike |
| egg | cup | boat |
| hay | dog | book |
| ice | fox | drum |
| knee | man | fish |
| pea | mop | hose |
| pie | pig | jump |
| sew | pin | ladder |
| tea | rat | lamp |
| toe | van | leaf |
| | | mask |
| | | nail |
| | | phone |
| | | quack |
| | | ski |
| | | star |
| | | turtle |
| | | yellow |
| | | zipper |

## Activity 13c: Elkonin Boxes—Sound Boxes

Prerequisite: Pushing Sounds Into Boxes, Activity 13b

Purpose: TLW hear all sounds in spoken words, isolate those sounds, think about the order of those sounds, and record those sounds.

Sample Standard Course of Study [SCOS] Competency Goal Objectives:

TLW demonstrate that spoken language is a sequence of identifiable speech sounds (adapted from *Language Arts: Kindergarten*, n.d.).

TLW segment the phonemes of one syllable words (adapted from *Language Arts: First Grade*, n.d.).

### Instructional Strategies

This activity should be taught for several days in a row using different examples.

### Grouping Strategies

| Whole Group | Small Group | Independent |
|---|---|---|
| Materials: <br><br> • Large rubber bands or thick piece of elastic <br> • Chart paper or board to pre-write Elkonin boxes <br> • Markers <br> • Picture cards <br> • Pocket chart to display picture cards <br> • If your board is magnetic, use round magnets as "markers/chips" as you push the sounds into boxes. <br><br> *Optional:* <br><br> *Elkonin boxes on overhead transparencies* <br><br> *Pictures for overhead representing the words you are stretching* <br><br> *Overhead projector* | Materials: <br><br> • "Thick" rubber bands or "skinny" balloons <br> • Chart paper or board to pre-write Elkonin boxes <br> • Index cards with Elkonin boxes <br> • Markers <br> • Picture cards <br> • Pocket chart to display picture cards <br> • "Markers/chips"* for manipulating while pushing sounds into boxes <br><br> *Optional:* <br><br> *Picture cards representing the words you are stretching* <br><br> *Pocket chart to display picture cards* | Materials: <br><br> • "Thick" rubber bands <br> • Index cards with Elkonin boxes <br> • "Markers/chips"* for manipulating while pushing sounds into boxes <br><br> *Optional:* <br><br> *Picture cards representing the words you are stretching* <br><br> *\*"markers/chips" may be game chips, milk carton tops, two-liter bottle tops, checkers, etc.* |

*Input/Modeling [Demonstrate]*

- Explain to the student(s) the purpose of the activity: ***"Now that you know how to hear how many sounds we hear in each word we stretch and how to push the sounds we hear into 'boxes,' today we are going to learn how to record those sounds in our boxes."***
- Show picture of a cat and say: ***"I have a picture of a cat. I am going to stretch the word 'cat' so that I can hear all the sounds in the word. /cccaaattt/."***
- ***"Now I am going to use my fingers to help me figure out how many sounds I hear in the word 'cat.'"*** This time as you slowly articulate, hold up one finger at a time as you isolate the sounds. (Make sure your fingers are facing the children so they see them go up from left to right.)
- ***"I have three fingers up, so I know that I hear three sounds in the word 'cat.'"***
- ***"I am going to draw three boxes up here on our chart/board."*** Draw three connecting boxes on the board and place a magnetic marker under each box. ***"I am going to put these three magnets here under each box. As I say the word 'cat' I am going to push the magnets up into the boxes as I say each sound slowly."***
- Demonstrate how to "push" the sounds into the boxes as you slowly articulate the word "cat."
- ***"Now, I need to record the sounds that I hear."*** Demonstrate how to "push" the sound in the boxes as you slowly articulate the word "cat."
- ***"I hear /t/ and I know that is the sound for the letter 't.' Let me push my sounds one more time to see where I will write the letter 't.'"*** Demonstrate how to "push" the sounds into the boxes as you slowly articulate the word "cat." Emphasis the /t/ sound.
- ***"That's it! Now I will write my letter 't' here in the last box, because that is where I heard that sound."***

*Guided Practice [Demonstrate]*

- ***"Now, let's try it together. Everybody stretch the word cat with me. Get your pretend rubber bands ready. OK, here we go, /cccaaattt/."***
- ***"Super! Raise you hand if you can tell me another sound we hear in the word 'cat.'"***
- ***"Yes. I do hear the /k/ sound. Raise your hand if you can tell me what letter represents that sound."*** Accept "k" as a response, but tell the student this time it is the other letter that makes the /k/ sound.
- ***"Now, we already have our three boxes, so as we say the word slowly, I would like _____ to come up here to show us how to push the sounds into the boxes until we find the box in which to put our letter 'c.'"*** Make sure the first child you call on is one who will be successful.
- ***"_____ thinks that we should write the letter 'c' in the first box here. If you agree, show me thumbs up. If you disagree, show me thumbs down."*** Check students' responses for understanding.
- ***"Fantastic! Let's record the letter 'c' in the first box."*** Follow the same procedures to finish recording the letters for the word 'cat' in the sound boxes.

*Independent Practice [Practice]*

When the children are in control of the task and beginning to record all of the sounds in sequence, you are ready to move to using letter boxes during their independent writing. Use one side of their journal as their "practice page." This will be the page on which they can draw their boxes and record the sounds they hear to support their journal writing.

*Check for Understanding [Prove]*

- ***"Let's try another word. Here is a picture of a dog. First, let's stretch the word together—/dddoooggg/. Now, let's use our fingers to count how many sounds are in the word 'dog', /dddoooggg/."*** Look around to check then call on a child who has the correct number of fingers up to tell the class how many sounds were in the word "dog."
- ***"Everybody, show me on your fingers how many boxes I need to draw on our board. Fantastic! You all are so smart! Yes, I do need three boxes."***
- Go back to the board where you have the three boxes and count the number of boxes with the students to confirm that you have three boxes already on the board.
- ***"Now, everybody slowly articulate the word 'dog' with me and pretend to push the sounds into the boxes as I push the sounds into the boxes up here."***
- ***"Who can raise their hand and tell me a sound you heard when you pushed the sounds into the boxes?"*** Typically, students will hear the last sound first, then the first sound, and finally the medial sound. Accept any order the students hear the sounds.
- Continue to push and record sounds as modeled during Guided Practice.
- Note the students who are having difficulty for pullout groups during independent work time.

| Differentiation | | |
|---|---|---|
| **Stage 1** | **Stage 2** | **Stage 3** |
| Words/pictures with two boxes | Words/pictures with three boxes | Words/pictures with four or more boxes |

## Sound Boxes

Sound boxes consist of one box for each sound in a word.

## Establishing the Task

Establish the task before you expect the children to understand and use boxes in their journals. Choose picture cards of words with sounds over which the children have control. Articulate slowly the word with the children. Do one or all of the following activities as you establish the task. They are listed in hierarchal order:

1. Model pushing the sounds into boxes as you both stretch the word. Do this several times.

2. Let the child stretch the word as the teacher pushes counters.

3. Let the child try pushing the counters as the teacher stretches the word.

4. Let the child push the counters and stretch the word independently.

When children are in control most of the time, you are ready to move to using sound boxes during journal writing.

Draw one box for each sound and let children push the counters into the boxes as they slowly articulate. Support students as needed by modeling or by guiding their hand. Let children record the sounds/letters they hear in the correct box *in any order.* Let them put "silent e" inside the box or outside the box—just be consistent. Remember, these are sound boxes, so if two letters make the sound, both letters go in the box. Remove the counters from the task as soon as possible and let children push with their finger. Move children from recording sounds in any order to recording sounds in sequence as soon as they are ready.

| sh | i | p |
|----|---|---|

As soon as the child can control most of the task and can record sounds in sequence the majority of the time with some support, begin to establish the task of transition boxes.

## Activity 13d: Elkonin Boxes—Transition Boxes

Prerequisite: Accurate and consistent use of sound boxes, Activity 13c

Purpose: TLW hear all sounds in spoken words, isolate those sounds, think about the order of those sounds, and record those sounds.

Sample Standard Course of Study [SCOS] Competency Goal Objectives:

TLW demonstrate that spoken language is a sequence of identifiable speech sounds (adapted from *Language Arts: Kindergarten*, n.d.).

TLW segment the phonemes of one and two syllable words.

TLW use phonic knowledge and basic patterns (e.g., *an, ee, ake*) to spell correctly three and four letter words (adapted from *Language Arts: First Grade*, n.d.).

## Grouping Strategies

| Whole Group | Small Group | Independent |
|---|---|---|
| Materials:<br><br>• Chart paper or board to pre-write Elkonin boxes<br>• Markers<br>• If your board is magnetic, use round magnets as "markers/chips" as you push the sounds into boxes.<br><br>*Optional:*<br><br>*Elkonin boxes on overhead transparencies*<br>*Overhead projector* | Materials:<br><br>• Chart paper or board to pre-write Elkonin boxes<br>• Index cards with Elkonin boxes<br>• Markers<br>• "Markers/chips"* for manipulating while pushing sounds into boxes | Materials:<br><br>• "Markers/chips"* for manipulating while pushing sounds into boxes<br><br>*\*"markers/chips" may be game chips, milk carton tops, two-liter bottle tops, checkers, etc.* |

### Instructional Strategies

This activity should be taught for several days in a row using different examples.

*Input/Modeling [Demonstrate]*

- Explain to the student(s) the purpose of the activity: **"Now that you know how to record sounds we hear in boxes, we are going to learn how to record the sound we hear in boxes when some sounds are represented by two letters."**
- **"Let's start with the word 'heavy.'"**
- **"I am going to use my fingers to help me figure out how many sounds I hear in the word 'heavy.'"** This time as you slowly articulate, hold up one finger at a time as you isolate the sounds. (Make sure your fingers are facing the children so they see them go up from left to right.)
- **"I have four fingers up, so I know that I hear four sounds in the word 'heavy.'"**
- **"I am going to draw four boxes up here on our chart/board."** Draw four connecting boxes on the board and place a magnetic marker under each box.
- **"Now, I know that in the second box there are two letters that make up that one sound, so I am going to draw a dashed line down the middle of the box."**
- **"I am still going to put these four magnets here, one under each box. As I say the word 'heavy' I am going to push the magnets up into the boxes and say the word slowly."**

- Demonstrate how to "push" the sounds into the boxes as you slowly articulate the word "heavy" and record the sounds your hear as you continue to think out loud.

### Guided Practice [Demonstrate]

- *"Now, let's try another one together. Everybody stretch the word 'steep' with me. Get your 'pretend' rubber bands ready. OK, here we go, /sstteeeepp/."*
- *"Good, now let's try to use our fingers to help us count how many sounds we hear in the word 'steep.' Get your fingers up, get ready, let's go . . . /sstteeeepp/."*
- *"Super!"*
- *"Now, we have to draw our four boxes. I know there are two letters representing the third sound, so I am going to draw a dashed line down the middle of that box."*
- *"As we say the word slowly, I would like _____ to come up here to show us how to push and record one of the sounds in the boxes."* Make sure the first child you call on is one who will be successful. Then call on several other children to try pushing the sounds into the boxes as the rest of the class slowly articulates the word "steep" and the correct letters are recorded.

### Independent Practice [Practice]

When the children are in control of the task and beginning to record all of the sounds in sequence, you are ready to move to using letter boxes during their independent writing. Use one side of their journal as their "practice page." This will be the page on which they can draw their boxes and record the sounds they hear to support their journal writing.

### Check for Understanding [Prove]

- Observe the children as they are writing and using sound boxes. Add transitional boxes (dashes) as needed for students to record the letters correctly. Support students as needed.
- Note the students who are having difficulty for pullout groups during independent work time.

### Differentiation

| Stage 1 | Stage 2 | Stage 3 |
| --- | --- | --- |
| Words with two or three boxes and one transitional box. | Words with three or four boxes and one or two transitional boxes. | Words with four or more boxes and two or more transitional boxes. |

### Transition Boxes

Transition boxes consist of one solid box per sound and a dotted line designating two letters for one box.

### Establish the Task

Establish the task by explaining the reason for the dotted lines.

Let the children slowly articulate and push the sounds into the boxes. Allow the students to record what they hear and prompt them to fill in the sounds/letters in sequential order. Let the students control the task as much as possible. You can support them by telling them the letters they don't hear and letting them write the letters in the proper box.

| h | e ┊ a | v | y |
|---|---|---|---|

When the children are able to hear sounds in sequence and are linking "chunks" of letter/sounds together, they are ready to move to letter boxes.

## Activity 13e: Elkonin Boxes—Letter Boxes

Prerequisite: Use of transition boxes and recording sounds in sequence, Activity 13d

Purpose: TLW hear all sounds in spoken words, isolate those sounds, and record those sounds in the order heard.

Sample Standard Course of Study [SCOS] Competency Goal Objectives:

TLW demonstrate that spoken language is a sequence of identifiable speech sounds (adapted from *Language Arts: Kindergarten*, n.d.).

TLW segment the phonemes of one and two syllable words.

TLW use phonic knowledge and basic patterns (e.g., *an, ee, ake*) to spell correctly three and four letter words (adapted from *Language Arts: First Grade*, n.d.).

## Grouping Strategies

| Whole Group | Small Group | Independent |
|---|---|---|
| Materials: <br><br> • Chart paper or board to pre-write Elkonin boxes <br> • Markers <br> • Wipe boards/paper <br><br> *Optional:* <br><br> *Blank overhead transparencies* <br> *Overhead projector* | Materials: <br><br> • Chart paper or board to pre-write Elkonin boxes <br> • Index cards with Elkonin boxes <br> • Markers <br> • Wipe boards/paper | Materials: <br><br> • Blank paper <br> • Pencils |

## Instructional Strategies

This activity should be taught for several days in a row using different examples.

*Input/Modeling [Demonstrate]*

- Explain to the student(s) the purpose of the activity: "Now that you know how to hear and record the sounds in words in sequence, you are ready to move on to using letter boxes to help you write new words."
- *"I am going to show you how we will use letter boxes to write words correctly. Let's begin with the word 'picnic.' Since you, as a student, do not know how to write that word, I am going to tell you how many boxes you need to record each letter in the word. We will need six boxes."*
- Draw six boxes on the paper/board.
- *"Now, instead of pushing the sounds into the boxes, I am going to just move my finger under the boxes as I slowly say the word 'picnic.'"*
- *"Finally, I am going to say the word slowly one more time, but this time I am going to record the sounds I hear as my finger passes under the boxes. Think aloud as you record each of the letters for the word 'picnic.'"*

*Guided Practice [Demonstrate]*

- *"Now, let's try one together. Everybody stretch the word 'jumps' with me. I know that you are going to need five boxes. Everyone draw five boxes on your paper/board."* Check students for accurate drawing of the five boxes and support as needed.
- *"Super!"*
- *"Now, as we say the word slowly, I would like you to record with me the letters of the sounds we hear in the boxes as we slide our finger under the boxes."*
- *"Raise your hand if you can tell me the first letter we will write in the first box."*

Make sure you call on a variety of students as you continue the process of recording all the sounds in the word "jumps" together.

*Independent Practice [Practice]*

When the children are in control of the task and beginning to record all of the sounds in sequence, you are ready to move to using letter boxes during their independent writing. Use one side of their journal as their "practice page." This will be the page on which they can draw their boxes and record the sounds they hear to support their journal writing.

*Check for Understanding [Prove]*

- Note the students who are having difficulty for pullout support groups during independent work time.

## Differentiation

| Stage 1 | Stage 2 | Stage 3 |
| --- | --- | --- |
| Teacher draws the boxes for the student to record the letters. | Teacher tells the student how many boxes they need to spell the word, and the student draws the boxes. | Boxes are needed occasionally for the student to spell most new words. |

### Letter Boxes

Letter boxes consist of one box per letter.

### Establish the Task

Establish the task by explaining there is now one box for every letter in the word. Encourage the child to slide his or her finger under the boxes as he or she records sounds in sequence. Prompt for independence, but give support when needed. Use boxes only as a support when needed to build spelling skills.

# Nonsense Word Fluency

*Phonics instruction is important because it leads to an understanding of the alphabetic principle—the systematic and predictable relationships between written letters and spoken sounds.*

National Institute for Literacy (2003)

Several different approaches to phonics instruction have been incorporated in these lessons including synthetic phonics, analytic phonics, analogy-based phonics, phonics through spelling, and onset-rime phonics instruction. These lessons were developed for teachers to use with their students in no particular sequential order. Activities 14–17 were developed as hands-on transitional activities from alphabetic knowledge to phonics instruction. Students practice going from letter to sound and sound to letter while participating in these beginning stages of synthetic phonics activities. More synthetic phonics lessons are found in Activities 18–20. Students learn how to convert letter combinations into sounds and how to blend the sounds into words. The rest of the activities (21–29) provide further experiences for the students to practice through analytical, analogy-based, and onset-rime phonics instruction.

## Improving Nonsense Word Fluency

Mrs. Walker's first-grade class included children performing at least two years below grade level. They were grouped together for intensive instruction so that they would reach benchmark level by the end of first grade on their DIBELS assessments. The students all lived below the poverty level, 70% were Limited English Proficient, and all had been enrolled in an American school for at least one year.

In the beginning of the school year, Mrs. Miller and the literacy teacher administered the DIBELS assessments. All 18 students scored 0 on their Nonsense Word Fluency Assessment. Since benchmark was 25 for that time of year and 50 for the midyear, the teachers knew immediate intervention was needed in establishing knowledge of sounds. The teachers introduced sounds to the class through the core program in place for the district and then provided supplemental teaching of the sounds in small groups using the sense of touch lessons and the letter sound Bingo activities. Once students had mastered several sounds, the teachers used the blending activities in small groups to help students learn to put the sounds together.

The teachers noticed in their small groups that a core group of five students— Martin, Maria, Lucero, Sara, and Marco—were learning the sounds and blending very quickly and were ready to move to a more advanced activity. In addition, the students were using the sounds very fluently in their writing. Mrs. Miller and the literacy teacher used Word Wheels and Flip Books to introduce the students to word families. In addition, the students used Slide-a-Word and Word Maker as reinforcement of building words during their center time. The students began by working with CVC words but then moved to more complex words/patterns as the year progressed.

These five students showed outstanding growth. By midyear, the students met benchmark on their Nonsense Word Fluency assessment in DIBELS. In addition, the remainder of the class received instruction with the same activities but moved at a more regular pace. Most (90%) of the class was on benchmark level (more than 50 sounds per minute) by the end of first grade. Both teachers believed that the students made this growth because of the intense small-group instruction.

Table 5.1   Mrs. Walker's "High Flyers" [Benchmark Assessments]

| Name | September NWF | January NWF |
|---|---|---|
| Martin | 0 | 65 |
| Maria | 0 | 70 |
| Lucero | 0 | 55 |
| Sara | 0 | 66 |
| Marco | 0 | 75 |

# Classroom Activities

## Activity 14: Distinguishing Letters/Sounds Using Sense of Touch

Purpose: The learner will [TLW] identify letters representing sounds using sense of touch.

Sample Standard Course of Study [SCOS] Competency Goal Objective:

TLW recognize and name uppercase and lowercase letters of the alphabet (adapted from *Language arts: Kindergarten*, n.d.).

### Grouping Strategies

| Whole Group | Small Group | Independent |
|---|---|---|
| Materials: | Materials: | Materials: |
| • Athletic sock with a cup placed inside | • Athletic sock with a cup placed inside | • Athletic sock with a cup placed inside |
| • Magnetic letters | • Magnetic letters | • Magnetic letters |
| • Sound/spelling picture cards | • Sound/spelling picture cards | • Chart to graph letters pulled HO14 |
| | | • Crayons/markers |
| *Optional* | *Optional* | • Sound/spelling picture cards matching the magnetic letters you are using |
| *Large chart to graph letters pulled* | *Medium-size chart to graph letters pulled* | |
| *Crayons/markers* | *Crayons/markers* | |

## Instructional Strategies

This activity is written so it may be adapted as new letters are introduced in your core reading program lessons.

*Input/Modeling [Demonstrate]*

- Explain to the student(s) the purpose of the activity: "Today we are going to use our sense of touch to identify some letters of the alphabet."
- Show students the sock-covered cup and explain the purpose of the activity: ***"I have placed some magnetic letters in this sock. I am using only the letters we have learned so far in our lessons."*** Point to the alphabet picture cards above your board and your alphabet chart.
- ***"We are going play a special game today. I am going to draw a picture card from this pile. Then I will let you slip your hand down in***

*the sock and try to find the magnetic letter that matches the first sound of the picture card. When you think you have found the letter you must not take your hand out of the sock until I tell you to do so. When I tell you it is OK, pull your hand and the letter out so we can see if you are correct. If we think you are correct, we will touch our nose. If we do not think you are correct, we will touch our knee."*

- *"Let me show you what I expect you to do."* As you show them what you expect, review the procedures aloud: *"If you think I am correct, touch your nose. If I am not correct, touch your knee. Good job!"*
- OPTIONAL: *"Now I am going to color in the box on my graph that is just above the letter/sound I identified. I am going to color in this box since I pulled the letter/sound ___."* Color in the correct box, modeling for the students what will be expected of them during independent work time.
- *"Remember, you cannot pull your letter out until I tell you to do so."*

### Guided Practice [Demonstrate]

- *"Now let's have some of you give it a try."*
- Call on several children to find the magnetic letter representing the letter name *or* letter sound you prompt them to find.
- OPTIONAL: Have the students color in the correct box on the class graph.
- Keep the materials ready for "filler" activities when you have a few minutes to spare.

### Independent Practice [Practice]

Place the materials in your ABC center for students to practice identifying letters/sounds using their sense of touch during independent work time. (For accountability purposes, students will need to work with a partner so the partner can check for accuracy.) Write the letters contained in the sock/cup along the bottom of the graph. (The letters will depend on which ones you have introduced to them in class.)

- The student will draw a picture card from the pile provided.
- Then the student will reach inside the sock to find the letter that matches the sound/spelling picture card.
- The student's partner will check if the student is correct.
- If correct, the students will complete the activity sheet, Handout 14, by coloring a block in the correct column on the graph each time they identify the correct letter.

### Check for Understanding [Prove]

- As the students signal, check for understanding.
- Note the students who are still having difficulty for pullout groups during independent work time.

## Differentiation

| Stage 1 | Stage 2 | Stage 3 |
|---|---|---|
| Supply students with only two different letters they have learned in their lessons. The letters you use should not be visually/tactilely similar. Have multiple copies of the letters. *Example:* s, S, s, M, m, m. | Supply students with no more than four different letters they have learned in their lessons. *Example:* S, s, M, m, A, a, p, P | Supply students with a variety of letters that they have been taught in their lessons. For best results, use no more than ten letters at a time as they perform the activity. |

## Attachment

- Letter Graph, Handout 14

# Handout 14

## Matching Sound to Letter

Name: _____    Date: _____

Complete the graph below by coloring in a box in the correct column as you correctly identify the letters chosen from the sock/cup.

| | | | My partner today was: |
|---|---|---|---|
| | | | _____ |
| | | | Sum up the activity |
| | | | |
| | | | |
| | | | |

# Activity 15a: Sound/Letter BINGO

> Purpose: The learner will [TLW] identify and mark *sound to letter* while playing a game, BINGO.
>
> Sample Standard Course of Study [SCOS] Competency Goal Objective:
>
> TLW demonstrate understanding of the sound of letters (adapted from *Language arts: Kindergarten*, n.d.).

## Instructional Strategies

K Teachers: Use only the alphabet picture cards and letter cards that have been introduced so far in your core reading program lessons.

Hint: Have other teachers create two or three BINGO cards, then photocopy them onto construction paper or cardstock to share in each classroom for a variety of boards.

*Input/Modeling [Demonstrate]*

- Explain the activity to the students: ***"Today we are going to play a game to help us practice identifying the letters that go with the sounds we have learned in our reading lessons."***
- ***"You already know how to play our game, but I have put a little 'twist' on it. I will briefly go over how we are going to play our game of BINGO today."***
- ***"First, I am going to put you with a partner. Then, I am going to give you and your partner a BINGO board with letters on it and some 'chips' for you to mark your card."***
- ***"I have a bag here with picture cards in it. I will draw a card from my bag and when I point to the card I want all of you to say the***

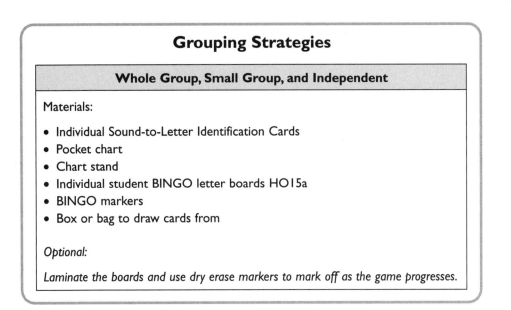

**Grouping Strategies**

| Whole Group, Small Group, and Independent |
|---|

Materials:

- Individual Sound-to-Letter Identification Cards
- Pocket chart
- Chart stand
- Individual student BINGO letter boards HO15a
- BINGO markers
- Box or bag to draw cards from

*Optional:*

*Laminate the boards and use dry erase markers to mark off as the game progresses.*

*beginning sound. Remember, wait until I point to the card! Let's try it.*" Keep practicing until all students respond only when you point to the picture card.

- *"Super! Now when I touch the picture card I want you to tell me the name of the letter it represents. Remember to wait until I point to the card! Don't let me trick you!"* Keep practicing until all students respond only when you point to the picture card.

- *"Fantastic! You all are so good at that! I really like the way you wait until I touch the card."*

- Display an example of a BINGO board on the overhead or hold one of them up for all of them to see then say: *"I need everybody's eyes up here. This is what your board may look like. All of you will have a different board, but they all will have letters on them."*

- *"I am going to draw a picture card from my bag and when I point to it, I want you to tell me the first sound of the picture."* Pull out a card, point to it and say: *"Sound."* Then point to it and say: *"Letter. Wow! Great job."*

- *"Now I need to look at my card and I need to find the letter that matches the picture card I drew from my bag. I can choose any letter in any box, but only one letter at a time. When I find the letter I want to cover, I will place my 'marker' on it."*

- *"The game continues until you have covered five letters in a row, either up and down, side to side, or diagonally. When you have covered five letters in a row, you and your partner will say, 'BINGO!'"*

*Guided Practice [Demonstrate]*

- Have each student take a partner; then pass out the materials they will need to play the game.

- *"Let's play a practice picture card. I am going to draw a card. Remember, do not say the sound or letter name until I point to it and say 'sound' or 'letter.'"*

- Draw a card from your bag. Hold it up so all students can see then point and say, *"Sound"* . . . point, *"Letter."*

- *"Now look on your card to see if you and your partner can find a letter that matches the picture card I drew from the bag."*

- *"Let's do one more like that together."* Follow the same procedures stated above.

*Independent Practice [Practice]*

Continue the game as time allows.

Option 1

1. Place the game pieces in the ABC center for groups of students to play the game.

2. One student is the teacher, while the others mark their cards.

*Check for Understanding [Prove]*

- Observe students as they participate in the activity and praise/correct as needed.

---

### Differentiation

| Stage 1 | Stage 2 |
|---|---|
| Play the game with partners so students can support each other. | Each child has his or her own BINGO card on which to play the game. |

---

## Attachments

- Blank BINGO card Handout 15a
- Sample BINGO cards using pictures from *Individual Sound and Letter Identification Card Examples* are provided. Use other clip art to create other cards.

# Handout 15a

## Sound and Letter Identification

| B | I | N | G | O |
|---|---|---|---|---|
|   |   |   |   |   |
|   |   |   |   |   |
|   |   |   |   |   |
|   |   |   |   |   |
|   |   |   |   |   |

# Individual Sound and Letter Identification Card Examples
## [Levels 1-3]

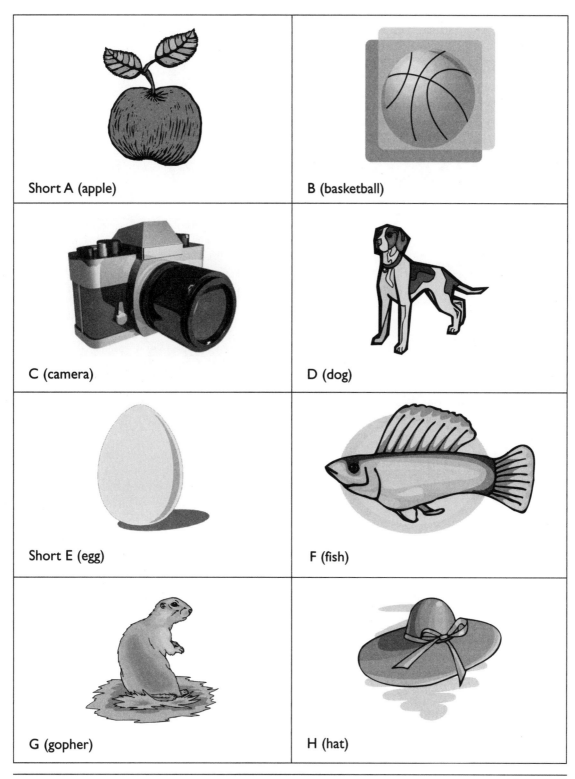

Short A (apple)

B (basketball)

C (camera)

D (dog)

Short E (egg)

F (fish)

G (gopher)

H (hat)

*(Continued)*

(Continued)

| | |
|---|---|
| Short I (igloo) | J (jump rope) |
| K (kite) | L (lion) |
| M (monkey) | N (net) |
| Short O (octopus) | P (present) |

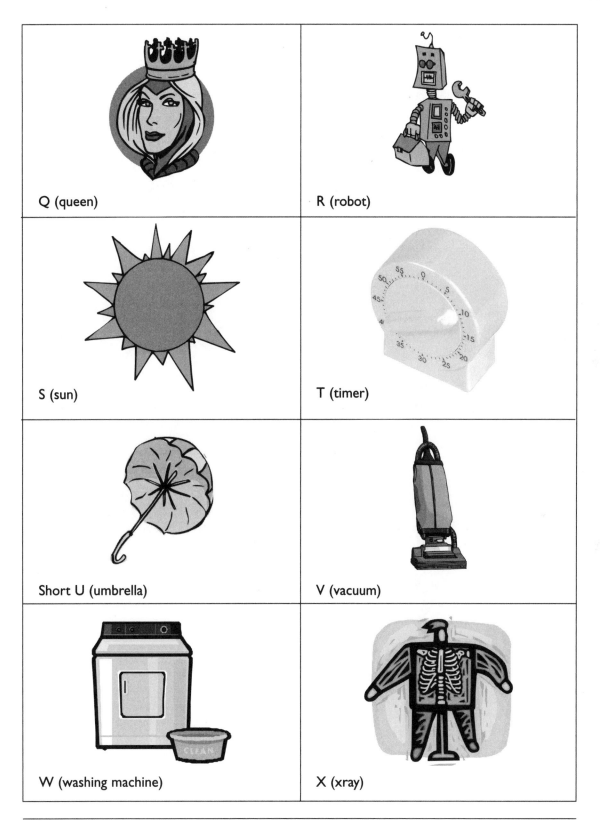

Q (queen)

R (robot)

S (sun)

T (timer)

Short U (umbrella)

V (vacuum)

W (washing machine)

X (xray)

*(Continued)*

(Continued)

Y (yoyo)

Z (zipper)

Long A (ape)

Long E (eagle)

Long I (ice cream)

Long O (ocean)

Long U (juice)

Sh (shell)

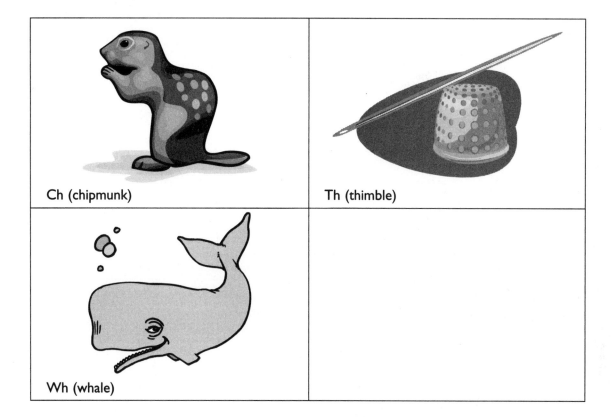

Ch (chipmunk)

Th (thimble)

Wh (whale)

# Activity 15b: Letter/Sound BINGO

Purpose: The learner will [TLW] identify and mark *letter to sound* while playing a game, BINGO.

Sample Standard Course of Study [SCOS] Competency Goal Objective:

TLW demonstrate understanding of the sound of letters (adapted from *Language arts: Kindergarten*, n.d.).

## Grouping Strategies

### Whole Group, Small Group, and Independent

Materials:

- Individual Sound/Spelling Cards
- Pocket chart
- Chart stand
- Individual Student Letter-to-Sound Identification BINGO boards
- BINGO markers
- Box or bag to draw cards from

*Optional:*

*Laminate the boards and use dry erase markers to mark off as the game progresses.*

## Instructional Strategies

K Teachers: Use only the picture cards and letter cards that have been introduced so far in your core reading program lessons.

Hint: If each teacher creates two or three BINGO cards, then you can photocopy them onto construction paper or cardstock to share among each classroom for a variety of boards.

*Input/Modeling [Demonstrate]*

- Explain the activity to the students: ***"Today we are going to play a game to help us practice identifying the sounds that go with the letters we have learned in our reading lessons."***
- ***"If you have ever played BINGO before, please raise your hand."***
- ***"Good, many of you already know how to play our game. I will briefly go over how we are going to play our game of BINGO today."***
- ***"First, I am going to put you with a partner. Then, I am going to give you and your partner a BINGO board with pictures on it and some 'chips' for you to mark your card."***
- ***"I have a bag here with letter cards in it. I will draw a card from my bag and when I point to the card I want all of you to name that***

*letter. Remember to wait until I point to the card! Let's try it."* Keep practicing until all students respond only when you point to the letter card.

- *"Super! Now when I touch the letter card I want you to tell me the sound of the letter. Remember to wait until I point to the card! Don't let me trick you!"* Keep practicing until all students respond only when you point to the letter card.
- *"Fantastic! You all are so good at that! I really like the way you wait until I touch the card."*
- Display an example of a BINGO board on the overhead or hold one of them up for all of them to see, then say: *"I need everybody's eyes up here. This is what your board may look like. All of you will have a different board, but they all will have pictures on them."*
- *"I am going to draw a card from my bag and when I point to it, I want you to tell me the name of the letter."* Pull out a card, point to it and say, *"Letter."* Then point to it and say, *"Sound."*
- *"Now I need to look at my card, and I need to find a picture that begins with the same sound as the letter I drew from my bag. I can choose any picture in any box, but only one picture at a time. When I find the picture I want to cover, I place my 'marker' on it."*
- *"The game continues until you have covered five pictures in a row, either up and down, side to side, or diagonally. When you have covered five pictures in a row, you and your partner will say, 'BINGO!'"*

### Guided Practice [Demonstrate]

- Have each student take a partner, then pass out the materials they will need to play the game.
- *"Let's play a practice letter. I am going to draw a letter. Remember, do not say the letter name or sound until I point to it and say 'letter' or 'sound.'"*
- Draw a card from your bag. Hold it up so all students can see, then point and say, *"Letter"* . . . point *"Sound."*
- *"Now look on your card and see if you and your partner can find a picture that begins with the letter I drew from the bag."*
- *"Let's do one more like that together."* Follow the same procedures stated above.

### Independent Practice [Practice]

Continue the game as time allows.

Option 1

1. Place the game pieces in the ABC center for groups of students to play the game.
2. One student is the teacher, while the others mark their cards.

### Check for Understanding [Prove]

- Observe students as they participate in the activity and praise/correct as needed.

## Differentiation

| Stage 1 | Stage 2 |
|---------|---------|
| Play the game with partners so students can support each other. | Each child has his or her own BINGO card on which to play the game. |

## Attachments

- Blank BINGO card Handout 15a
- Sample BINGO cards using pictures from *Individual Sound and Letter Identification Card Examples* are provided. Use other clip art to create other cards.

## Activity 16: Sound Identification Game

Purpose: The learner will [TLW] confirm or discount sound-to-letter matches.

Sample Standard Course of Study [SCOS] Competency Goal Objective:

TLW demonstrate understanding of the sound of letters (adapted from *Language Arts: Kindergarten*, n.d.).

## Grouping Strategies

| Whole Group | Small Group | Independent |
|-------------|-------------|-------------|
| Materials:<br><br>• Chart tablet displays<br>• Markers<br>• Chart stand<br><br>*Optional:*<br><br>*Overhead displays* | Materials:<br><br>• Chart tablet displays<br>• Markers<br>• Chart stand<br><br>*Optional:*<br><br>*Put student pages together to form a group book.* | Materials:<br><br>• Accountability sheet<br><br>*Optional:*<br><br>*Keep student sheets separate and create a "student" book when all pages are complete.* |

## Instructional Strategies

*Input/Modeling [Demonstrate]*

- Explain the activity to the students: ***"Today we are going to do a quick review of some of the sounds we have learned so far this year in our reading lessons, and I need your help."***

- Display a chart tablet with a list of letters displayed in a row. Use only letters you have taught and one new letter. Intersperse the new letter several times on the page. (See Transparency 16 for an example.)
- *"I have a list of letters here on my chart. I am going to point to one letter at a time and ask you a question. You will need to answer either 'yes' or 'no' as I snap my fingers."*
- *"Let me show you what I mean."* Point to the first letter on the chart and ask, *"Is this an /m/?"* Snap your fingers and say, *"Yes."*

*Guided Practice [Demonstrate]*

- *"Now you try it with me."* Point to the first letter on the chart again, ask the question, and snap your fingers until everyone understands the task.
- *"Great job! Let's try some more."* Point to the rest of the letters in the row and ask the same question, *"Is this an /m/?"* Snap your fingers and wait for their response. Praise as needed.

*Independent Practice [Practice]*

1. Pass out Handout 16 and explain the activity to the students.

2. They are to circle all of the "m"s on the page.

*Check for Understanding [Prove]*

- Observe the students as you go through the activity.
- Call on several students to respond independently.

### Differentiation

| Stage 1 | Stage 2 | Stage 3 |
|---|---|---|
| Use only two letters on the chart/transparency/handout. | Use three letters on the chart/transparency/handout. | Use four or more letters on the chart/transparency/handout. |

- Check Handout 16 and reteach as needed during independent work time as needed.

## Attachments

- Transparency Overhead Transparency 16
- Accountability Sheet Handout 16

# Transparency 16

## Sound of the Day: Is This an "m"?

EXAMPLE ONLY

*"Is this an 'm'?"*

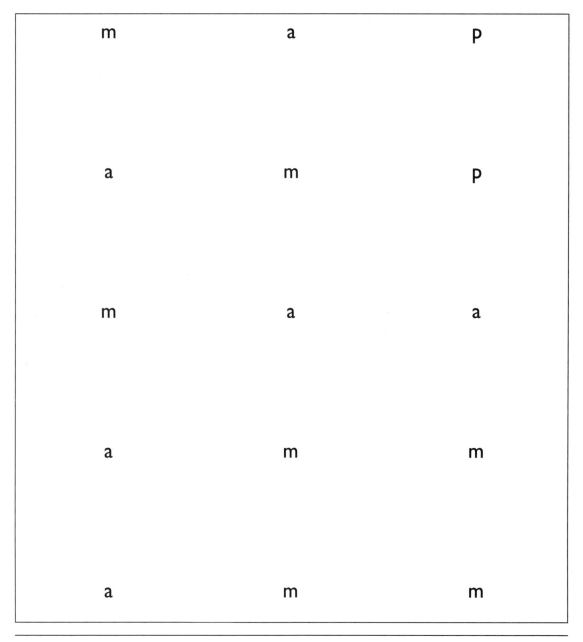

|  |  |  |
|---|---|---|
| m | a | p |
| a | m | p |
| m | a | a |
| a | m | m |
| a | m | m |

# Handout 16

## Sound of the Day

*Name:* _____ *Date:* _____

Circle all of the letters that represent our "Sound of the Day."

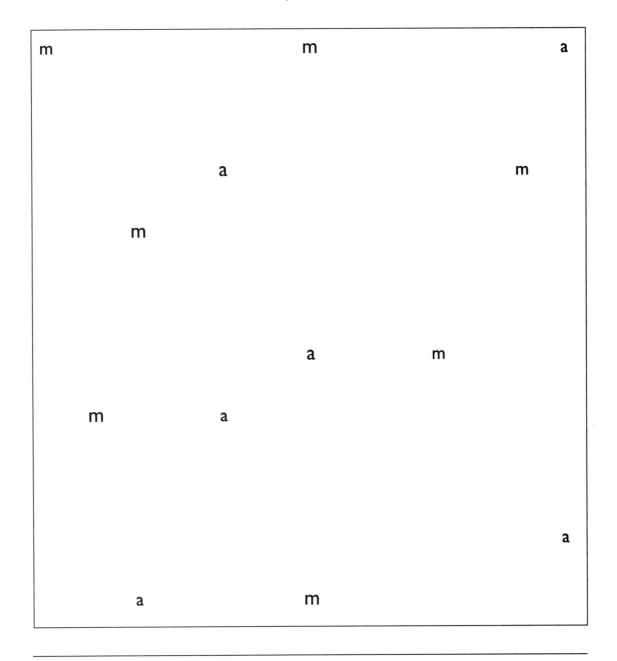

# Activity 17: Making and Breaking Using Magnetic Letters

Purpose: The learner will [TLW] blend sounds to create words.

Sample Standard Course of Study [SCOS] Competency Goal Objectives:

TLW demonstrate that spoken language is a sequence of identifiable speech sounds (adapted from *Language Arts: Kindergarten*, n.d.).

TLW segment the phonemes of one syllable words (adapted from *Language Arts: First Grade*, n.d.).

## Instructional Strategies

*Tips for Using Magnetic Letters*

1. Magnetic letters are not used to learn specific words, but rather to show how words work.

2. Magnetic letter activities should last no more than two to three minutes.

3. The teacher should demonstrate first and verbalize what she or he is doing.

### Grouping Strategies

| Whole Group | Small Group | Independent |
|---|---|---|
| Materials: | Materials: | Materials: |
| • Magnetic letters<br>• Overhead projector | • Magnetic letters<br>• Vertical metal surface | • Magnetic letters<br>• Vertical metal surface |

4. Students should be actively involved during the activities and should use both hands when manipulating the letters.

5. Magnetic letter activities should begin with what the child knows.

6. A vertical surface should be used for activities.

7. Three examples are enough.

*Input/Modeling [Demonstrate]*

- *"Today we are going to use magnetic letters to make some words that we are reading in our decodable books."*
- *"I am going to place the three letters that I need up here on our overhead projector."* Use only the letters you need to "make" your word for the day.
- *"Now, I am going to use the letters to make the word _____. Let's see. First, I hear / /, so I am going to place the letter ____ at the top left side of the board. Next, I hear / / so I am going to place the letter*

_____*right beside the letter* _____. *Notice that I am not leaving any space between my two letters. That is because when we write words, we do not leave spaces between the letters that make up those words. Finally, I hear  / /  so I am going to place my last letter,* _____, *right here at the end of my word."*

- *"When I read my word the fast way, I run my finger under the word and say it quickly. But sometimes, if I am not sure how to read the new word, I need to move my letters apart like this* (demonstrate how you separate the letter in the words), *so I can blend my sounds together in order to read the word. I call this 'breaking' a word apart."*

- Demonstrate slow articulation of the letters spaced apart as you slowly run you finger under all the letters.

- Say, *"Now that we have read our word slowly, I am going to put my letters back together. I call this 'making' a word. I will read the word the fast way again."* Demonstrate how you run your finger quickly under the word as you say it.

## Guided Practice [Demonstrate]

- Segment and blend several new decodable words found in the reading books for the day.
- Call on different students to "break" and "make" the unknown words following the procedures outlined above.

## Independent Practice [Practice]

Allow students who need hands-on activities to use the magnetic letters to make and break apart words during their reading of the decodable books.

## Check for Understanding [Prove]

- Observe and note which students are having difficulty with the concept of making and breaking words as you work with the class.
- Reteach during independent work time as needed.

### Differentiation

*See attachment for more specific information on each of the stages mentioned below.

| Stage 1 | Stage 2 | Stage 3 |
|---------|---------|---------|
| Use only CVC words. | Use only word family words. | Use only prefixes, suffixes, compound words, and endings added to known words. |

## Attachment

- Making and Breaking Using Magnetic Letters Handout 17(a–b)

# Handout 17a

## Making and Breaking Using Magnetic Letters: Scaffolding Students' Learning

*Establishing the Task*

When **establishing the task**, *always* begin with a known word. This gives the students a way to link what they know to what you want them to learn about making and breaking words. **Remember**, *no more than three examples are necessary for students to understand the task and to keep students engaged in the activity. Avoid any examples that children are unlikely to encounter.*

*Making and Breaking Known Words*

Have the child **make and break the KNOWN word** several times. Follow the procedures outlined above by separating the letters, not mixing them up. The purpose is not to spell the words, but to learn to segment and blend new words.

*Making and Breaking Known Words to Unknown Words*

When the student understands the concept of making and breaking words, you are ready to move to the next step of **generating from known words to unknown words** using magnetic letters.

The teacher selects very easy and familiar words, such as "no" and "go," and provides only the letters needed for the activity. Then the teacher asks the child to construct the third word "so" and to read them all.

Always place the words in a column on the vertical surface so the students can benefit most from the activity.

The teacher may also select known words for **initial consonant substitution**. For example, the student knows the words "can" and "man," but does not know the word "pan." The teacher would prompt the student to use only the letters provided to make the words "can" and "man," then she would ask the child to use the remaining letters to create the word "pan."

Once that is established, the teacher will not need the letters to create all three words, but will keep the same "family" part and change only the onset to create the new words.

Possible Teaching Points

| -at | -ig | -e | -n | -op |
|-----|-----|-----|-----|-----|
| cat | big | me | an | mop |
| sat | pig | be | in | hop |
| fat | wig | we | on | pop |
| mat | | she | | stop |
| hat | | he | | |
| bat | | | | |

# Handout 17b

## Making and Breaking Using Prefixes, Suffixes, Compound Words, and Endings

| -ay | -ight | -in | -ot | -un |
|------|-------|-----|-----|-----|
| play | night | win | not | fun |
| day | right | pin | hot | run |
| say | light | tin | got | sun |
| way | sight | fin | rot | bun |
| may | fight | | pot | |

In order to best teach making and breaking of "chunks," you will need to glue/tape the magnetic letters needed to form the chunks. For example, if you are adding the ending "ing" to known words, glue/tape the letters I-N-G together so the letters act as a single unit of sound. The same goes for diphthongs and digraphs.

Possible Teaching Points

| Prefixes | Suffixes | Compound Words | Endings |
|----------|----------|----------------|---------|
| re-<br>pre- | -able<br>-ble | today<br>cowboy<br>away<br>into | -ing<br>-ly<br>-s<br>-es<br>-ies<br>-y |

*Teaching for Independence*

The following procedures will help lead the child to more independent problem solving ranging from the most teacher support to the least teacher support (scaffolding).

1. Teacher supplies the letters and/or models.

2. Teacher substitutes onsets.

3. Child substitutes onsets.

4. Teacher substitutes rimes.

5. Child substitutes rimes.

6. Child thinks of other known words.

7. Child makes up other words that are new to him.

# Activity 18a: Blending (VC)

Purpose: The learner will [TLW] blend chunks of (VC) letters.

Sample Standard Course of Study [SCOS] Competency Goal Objectives:

TLW demonstrate that spoken language is a sequence of identifiable speech sounds.

TLW demonstrate understanding that the sequence of letters in the written word represents the sequence of sounds in the spoken word.

TLW demonstrate understanding of the sounds of letters and understanding that words begin and end alike (onset and rimes).

TLW recognize most beginning consonant letter-sound associations in one syllable words (adapted from *Language Arts: Kindergarten*, n.d.).

TLW demonstrate decoding skills by using phonics knowledge of sound-letter relationships to decode regular one syllable words when reading words and text (adapted from *Language Arts: First Grade*, n.d.).

## Grouping Strategies

### Whole Group and Small Group

Materials:

- Chart tablet displays
- Chart stand
- Overhead projector
- Magnetic letters

*Optional:*

*Overhead letters*

*Pointer*

## Instructional Strategies

*Input/Modeling [Demonstrate]*

- Explain the activity to the students: ***"Today we are going to blend some of the 'sounds' we have learned so far this year in our reading lessons, and I need your help."***
- Display the chart tablet with the list of letters displayed in a row.
- ***"I have a list of letters here on my chart. I am going to point to each letter as I say its sound."***
- ***"Next, I am going to use two of these letters to blend some make-believe words. Let me show you what I mean. If I take the letter 'a' and the letter 'p' and place them beside each other like this, I can blend the sounds together to create a make-believe word."*** **Point to each letter and slide your finger under the 'word' as you say**

*the following: "I know 'a' makes the /a/ sound and 'p' makes the /p/ sounds, but when I blend them together they say /ap/."*

*Guided Practice [Demonstrate]*

- *"Now you try it with me. When I point to the letter I want you to say the sound, but when I slide my finger under the letters, I want you to blend the sounds and tell me the new 'word.'"* Point to the "a" and have the children give you that sound on cue. Point to the "p" and have the children give you that sound on cue, then say, *"Now, get ready, I am going to slide my finger under the whole thing. Ready—blend."* Keep practicing the following procedures until they are well established by all students.

- *"Great job! Let's try some more."* Choose another group of VC "words" to blend following the above procedures.

*Check for Understanding [Prove]*

- Observe the students as you go through the activity.
- Call on several students to respond independently.
- Reteach during independent work time as needed.

## Differentiation

| Stage 1 | Stage 2 | Stage 3 |
|---|---|---|
| Use only the sounds/letters the students have been taught to blend VC "words." | Use only the sounds/letters that students have been taught to blend CVC "words." | Use only the sounds/letters that students have been taught to blend CVC and other, actual words. |

# Activity 18b: Blending (CVC)

Purpose: The learner will [TLW] blend chunks of (CVC) letters.

Sample Standard Course of Study [SCOS] Competency Goal Objectives:

TLW demonstrate that spoken language is a sequence of identifiable speech sounds.

TLW demonstrate understanding that the sequence of letters in the written word represents the sequence of sounds in the spoken word.

TLW demonstrate understanding of the sounds of letters and understanding that words begin and end alike (onset and rimes).

TLW recognize most beginning consonant letter-sound associations in one syllable words (adapted from *Language arts: Kindergarten*, n.d.).

TLW demonstrate decoding skills by using phonics knowledge of sound-letter relationships to decode regular one syllable words when reading words and text (adapted from *Language Arts: First Grade*, n.d.).

## Instructional Strategies

*Input/Modeling [Demonstrate]*

- Explain the activity to the students: ***"Today we are going to blend some of the 'sounds' we have learned so far this year in our reading lessons, and I need your help."***
- Display the chart tablet with the list of letters displayed in a row.
- ***"I have a list of letters here on my chart. I am going to point to each letter as I say its sound."***
- ***"Next, I am going to use three of these letters to blend some make-believe words. Let me show you what I mean. If I take the letters 'p,' and 'a,' and the letter 's' and place them beside each other like this, I can***

---

### Grouping Strategies

| **Whole Group and Small Group** |
|---|

Materials:

- Chart tablet displays
- Chart stand
- Overhead projector
- Magnetic letters

*Optional:*

*Overhead letters*

*Pointer*

---

***blend the sounds together to create a make-believe word."*** Point to each letter and slide your finger under the "word" as you say the following: ***"I know 'p' makes the /p/ sound, the 'a' makes the /a/ sound, and 's' makes the /s/ sound, but when I blend them together they say /pas/."***

*Guided Practice [Demonstrate]*

- ***"Now you try it with me. When I point to the letter, I want you to say the sound, but when I slide my finger under the letters, I want you to blend the sounds and tell me the new 'word.'"*** Point to the "a" and have the children give you that sound on cue, point to the "p" and have the children give you that sound on cue, then say, ***"Now, get ready, I am going to slide my finger under the whole thing. Ready—blend."*** Keep practicing the following procedures until they are well established by all students.
- ***"Great job! Let's try some more."*** Choose another group of CVC "words" to blend following the above procedures.

*Check for Understanding [Prove]*

- Observe the students as you go through the activity.
- Call on several students to respond independently.
- Reteach during independent work time as needed.

## Differentiation

| Stage 1 | Stage 2 | Stage 3 |
|---------|---------|---------|
| Use only the sounds/letters the students have been taught to blend VC "words." | Use only the sounds/letters that students have been taught to blend CVC "words." | Use only the sounds/letters that students have been taught to blend CVC and other, actual words. |

## Activity 19: Sorting Beginning Consonant Sounds

Purpose: The learner will [TLW] apply knowledge of initial consonant sounds.

Sample Standard Course of Study [SCOS] Competency Goal Objectives:

TLW develop spelling strategies and skills by analyzing sounds (adapted from *Language Arts: Kindergarten,* n.d.).

TLW demonstrate decoding and word recognition strategies and skills (adapted from *Language Arts: First Grade,* n.d.).

## Grouping Strategies

| Whole Group | Small Group | Independent |
|-------------|-------------|-------------|
| Materials:<br><br>• Mounted pictures or objects that represent items beginning with two initial consonants previously learned<br>• Two milk containers with the tops cut off. Label with a consonant symbol on each container. (Hint: to reuse containers, simply use Velcro to attach letters on tag board to the container.)<br>• Number each picture for self-checking purposes on accountability sheets.<br>• Accountability sheets HO19 | Materials:<br><br>• Mounted pictures or objects that represent items beginning with two initial consonants previously learned<br>• Two milk containers with the tops cut off. Label with a consonant symbol on each container. (Hint: to reuse containers, simply use Velcro to attach letters on tag board to the container.)<br>• Number each picture for self-checking purposes on accountability sheets.<br>• Accountability sheets HO19 | Materials:<br><br>• Mounted pictures or objects that represent items beginning with two initial consonants previously learned<br>• Two milk containers with the tops cut off. Label with a consonant symbol on each container. (Hint: to reuse containers, simply use Velcro to attach letters on tag board to the container.)<br>• Number each picture for self-checking purposes on accountability sheets.<br>• Accountability sheets HO19<br><br>*Optional:*<br><br>*Picture cards, construction paper, scissors, glue sticks* |

### Instructional Strategies

*Input/Modeling [Demonstrate]*

- Explain to the students the purpose of the activity (sorting beginning consonant sounds).
- Pick up one of the picture/objects and say: ***"This is a picture of a _____. What sound do I hear at the beginning of that word? I hear a _____. Because I hear the sound _____, I am going to place it in the carton that is labeled _____."***
- Using a picture/object that represents the other consonant sound being compared, use the same procedure as above.

*Guided Practice [Demonstrate]*

- Explain to the students that you will practice this with them. They will fill in the blank when you pause using the sentence pattern used in the modeling stage.

*Independent Practice [Practice]*

Place the materials in your ABC center for students to practice the activity during independent work time. For accountability purposes, the teacher may use the accountability sheets or have the students paste the picture cards onto construction paper sorted into the two consonant sound groups.

*Check for Understanding [Prove]*

- As the students are calling out the missing information, check for those who seem unsure or hesitant. Note to keep them for pullout during independent work time.

### Attachment

- Accountability Sheet Handout 19

### Differentiation

| Stage 1 | Stage 2 | Stage 3 |
|---------|---------|---------|
| For students in this stage, the teacher should focus on only using two consonant sounds. | For students in this stage, the teacher should have the students sort more than two consonant sounds at one time. For an additional challenge, students can label the pictures using the sounds they know on their accountability sheets. | Students in this stage should be focusing on sorting blends and digraphs. For an additional challenge, students can label the pictures using the sounds they know on their accountability sheets. |

# Handout 19

## Sorting Beginning Consonant Sounds

Name: _____     Date: _____

Directions: After you sort the letters into the carton, write the numbers on the back of the pictures in the correct column below.

| Letter _____ | Letter _____ |
|---|---|
|  |  |
|  |  |
|  |  |
|  |  |
|  |  |
|  |  |
|  |  |
|  |  |
|  |  |

# Activity 20: Sound Line

Purpose: The learner will [TLW] identify letter-sound correspondences through pictures.

Sample Standard Course of Study [SCOS] Competency Goal Objective:

TLW develop spelling strategies and skills by analyzing sounds (adapted from *Language Arts: Kindergarten,* n.d.).

## Grouping Strategies

| Whole Group | Small Group | Independent |
|---|---|---|
| Materials:<br><br>• Rope<br>• Clothespins with uppercase and lowercase letters on them<br>• Mounted pictures on tag board that represent the sounds being studied (Teacher can choose how many consonants to include on the Sound Line.) | Materials:<br><br>• Rope<br>• Clothespins with uppercase and lowercase letters on them<br>• Mounted pictures on tag board that represent the sounds being studied (Teacher can choose how many consonants to include on the Sound Line.)<br><br>(See appendix for various pictures) | Materials:<br><br>• Rope<br>• Clothespins with uppercase and lowercase letters on them<br>• Mounted pictures on tag board that represent the sounds being studied (Teacher can choose how many consonants to include on the Sound Line.)<br><br>*Optional:*<br><br>*Paper*<br><br>*Crayons* |

## Instructional Strategies

*Input/Modeling [Demonstrate]*

- Explain to the students the purpose of the activity (identifying beginning consonant sounds).
- Pick up one of the pictures and say: ***"This is a picture of a _____. What sound do I hear at the beginning of that word? I hear a _____. Because I hear the sound _____, I am going to attach it to the clothespin that is labeled with the letter_____."***
- Repeat using a picture that represents another consonant sound.

*Guided Practice [Demonstrate]*

- Explain to the students that you will practice this with them. They will fill in the blank when you pause using the sentence pattern used in the modeling stage.

*Independent Practice [Practice]*

Place the materials in your ABC center for students to practice the activity during independent work time. For accountability purposes, students record their sound line onto paper (see attachment; teacher can modify as needed) recording both the letters/sounds on the line as well as drawing the corresponding picture underneath it.

*Check for Understanding [Prove]*

- As the students are calling out the missing information, check for those who seem unsure or hesitant. Note to keep them for pullout during independent work time.

### Differentiation

| Stage 1 | Stage 2 | Stage 3 |
|---------|---------|---------|
| Students in this stage can focus on two or three initial consonant sounds. | Students in this stage can focus on five or six initial consonant sounds. | Students in this stage can focus on blends and digraphs. |

## Attachment

- Blank Sound Line Accountability Sheet Handout 20

# Handout 20

## Sound Line

Name: _____     Date: _____

Directions: After you have completed your sound line using the clothespins and rope, record your answers below. Put the letter on the line and the matching picture in the box above it.

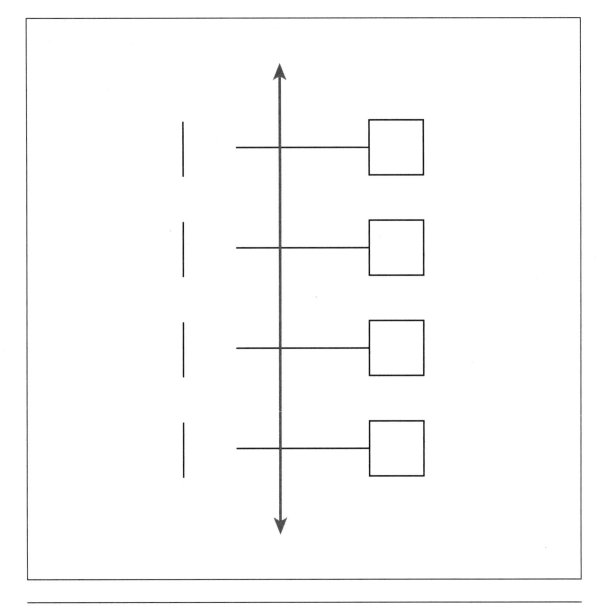

## Activity 21: Word Wheels

Purpose: The learner will [TLW] use phonics knowledge of sound-letter relationships to decode regular one syllable words when reading words.

Sample Standard Course of Study [SCOS] Competency Goal Objective:

TLW demonstrate decoding and word recognition strategies and skills (adapted from *Language Arts: First Grade*, n.d.).

*To Make a Word Wheel:* Using two pieces of different colored construction paper, construct two circles of the same size. Label the outer area of one of the circles with consonants (see below on diagram). Cut a small window (see below on diagram) out of the second circle and label the phonogram being studied on the second circle. Attach the two circles together with a brass fastener. The circles should rotate (see diagram below).

### Grouping Strategies

| Whole Group | Small Group | Independent |
|---|---|---|
| Materials:<br><br>• Large demo Word Wheel with same consonants and phonogram (see example below)<br>• Transparency of accountability sheet<br><br>(see attached phonogram list) | Materials:<br><br>• Word Wheels that contain a phonogram (e.g., -at) and a circle of consonants<br>• Pencils | Materials:<br><br>• Word Wheels that contain a phonogram (e.g., -at) and a circle of consonants<br>• Crayons<br>• Pencils<br>• Accountability sheet for students to record their work |

# Word Wheels

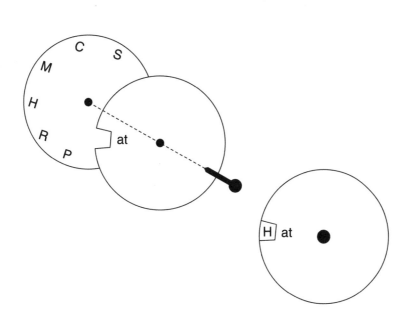

## Instructional Strategies

*Input/Modeling [Demonstrate]*

- Explain to students the purpose of the activity: (blending sounds to make a word)
- Point to the large phonogram and say, **"Sound /a/, sound /t/, blend them together /at/."** Moving the wheel so that a consonant shows beside the phonogram, say, **"This is the letter (h). It makes the sound /h/. When I put it with "at" I get the word /hat/."**
- Continue modeling with two more of the consonants.

*Guided Practice [Demonstrate]*

- Pass out the Word Wheels to groups of students. Using the same sentence structure as above, have students practice with other group members using the remainder of the consonants.

*Independent Practice [Practice]*

Before independent work time, show students the accountability sheet. Explain to them that as they make a word, they will write it on their accountability sheet. In order to check for understanding and meaning of the blended word children will draw a picture that represents the word made.

*Check for Understanding [Prove]*

- As the students are working in groups, check for correct blending.
- Note the students who are having difficulty for pullout groups during independent work time.

### Differentiation

| Stage 1 | Stage 2 | Stage 3 |
|---|---|---|
| Students in this stage might focus only on making CVC words with the phonogram being studied. | Students in this stage might focus on using blends and digraphs to form words with the phonogram being studied. | Students in this stage might focus on using three-letter blends combined with the phonogram being studied. |

## Attachment

- Accountability Sheet Handout 21

## List of Possible Phonograms for This Activity

| AT | AN | AD | AG | OP | OG |
|------|------|------|------|------|------|
| cat | can | dad | bag | hop | dog |
| fat | fan | sad | flag | top | log |
| hat | pan | mad | rag | mop | jog |
| mat | man | pad | tag | pop | frog |
| sat | van | wag | | | |
| bat | | | | | |
| rat | | | | | |
| pat | | | | | |

| ET | UG | Blends | Digraphs |
|------|------|--------|----------|
| net | bug | br, bl | th |
| jet | jug | st, sl, sk, sp, sn, sm, sw | ch |
| pet | mug | dr | sh |
| wet | tug | fr, fl | wh |
| rug | tr, thr | ph | |
| gr, gl | | | |
| pl, pr, | | | |
| cl, cr | | | |
| scr, str | | | |

# Handout 21

## Word Wheels

Name: _____     Date: _____

Directions: After you create a word on your word wheel, record the word on a line and then illustrate that word beside it.

1. _____

2. _____

3. _____

4. _____

5. _____

6. _____

7. _____

8. _____

## Activity 22: Flip Books

Purpose: The learner will [TLW] apply knowledge of initial consonant sounds as well as phonogram patterns to make new words.

Sample Standard Course of Study [SCOS] Competency Goal Objectives:

TLW develop spelling strategies and skills by analyzing sounds (adapted from *Language Arts: Kindergarten*, n.d.).

TLW demonstrate decoding and word recognition strategies and skills (adapted from *Language Arts: First Grade*, n.d.).

*To Make Flip Books:* Using construction paper, assemble pages horizontally and staple on left-hand side. On all but the last page, cut out a small rectangle out of the upper right-hand corner. On that corner of last page, label the phonogram that is being studied.

### Instructional Strategies

*Input/Modeling [Demonstrate]*

- Explain to the students the activity's purpose (using consonant sounds to build words in a book).
- Using the teacher Flip Book, show the students how the book is set up. Explain that your book will focus on -at words. Explain that their books will focus on a different pattern, but that they will help you with your book first.
- Have students brainstorm all of the -at words they know (e.g., hat, rat, bat, mat, etc. . . .). Show students how to record the initial consonant beside the phonogram on each page. Eventually show how each page has a different consonant, but still has the same word ending. After each page has a word on it, students go back and draw a picture to match the word they created. Ask students what patterns they notice in the words.

### Grouping Strategies

| Whole Group | Small Group | Independent |
|---|---|---|
| Materials:<br><br>• Teacher Flip Books (see directions and diagram below)<br>• Pencils<br>• Crayons | Materials:<br><br>• Preassembled Flip Books (see directions and diagram below)<br>• Pencils<br>• Crayons | Materials:<br><br>• Preassembled Flip Books (see directions and diagram below)<br>• Pencils<br>• Crayons |

# Flip Books

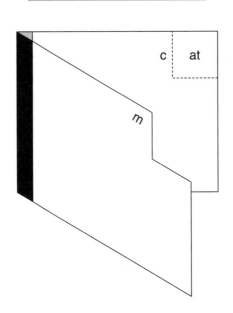

*Guided Practice [Demonstrate]*

- Explain to the students that you will practice this with them. They will complete one together in pairs using the teacher's choice of phonogram.

*Independent Practice [Practice]*

Place the materials in your ABC center for students to complete the activity during independent work time. Phonograms for study can be tailored to each child's needs (see Differentiation chart below). Students should go back and underline the phonogram on each page. Students can read aloud their "word" books to peers if time allows. This will aid in word fluency development.

*Check for Understanding [Prove]*

- As the students are working together, check for those who seem unsure or hesitant. Note to keep them for pullout during independent work time.

## Differentiation

| Stage 1 | Stage 2 | Stage 3 |
|---------|---------|---------|
| Students in this stage can create CVC words using the phonogram chosen by the teacher. They should include an illustration of the words. (e.g., mat, cat, hat, bat) | Students in this stage can create CVC words using the assigned phonogram. In addition, these students can write a sentence on each page using the words they have created (with a picture). | Students in this stage can create words using the assigned phonogram with blends and digraphs. In addition, these students can write a sentence on each page using the words they have created (with a picture). (e.g., ship, whip, chip, drip, trip) |

# Activity 23: Slide-a-Word

Purpose: The learner will [TLW] will create, list, read, and illustrate CVC words.

Sample Standard Course of Study [SCOS] Competency Goal Objectives:

TLW develop spelling strategies and skills by analyzing sounds (adapted from *Language Arts: Kindergarten,* n.d.).

TLW demonstrate decoding and word recognition strategies (adapted from *Language Arts: First Grade,* n.d.).

## Grouping Strategies

| Whole Group | Small Group | Independent |
|---|---|---|
| Materials:<br><br>• Word Slide (see directions and sample below)<br>• Paper<br>• Pencil<br>• Crayons<br>• Transparency of Accountability sheet HO23 | Materials:<br><br>• Word Slide (see directions and sample below). One is needed for each pair of students. | Materials:<br><br>• Word Slide (see directions and sample below)<br>• Paper<br>• Pencil<br>• Crayons<br>• Accountability sheet HO23 |

*Teacher Preparation for Slide-a-Word:* Cut a piece of tag board or poster board into strips 8½ by 2½ inches. Using a razorblade, cut a pair of horizontal slits on each end 1½ inches apart. In the center, write a vowel. Cut two 12 by 1½ inch strips for each slider. Thread them through the slits at each end and write a variety of consonants, blends, or digraphs that have previously been taught. Then, turn the strips over and write other beginning and ending sounds on the back. See below.

# Teacher Preparation
# for Slide-a-Word

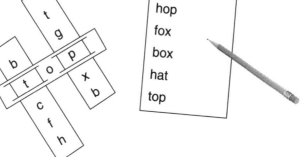

### Instructional Strategies

*Input/Modeling [Demonstrate]*

- Explain to the students the purpose of the activity (building words)
- Model for students how to use the slider. Say, ***"I am sliding the paper strips and I have the letters t-o-p. They make the sounds /t/ /o/ /p/. That word is top. I will record it on my sheet. To show that I know what this word says, I will draw a picture of a top beside the word that I wrote."***
- Repeat with another word created by the slider.

*Guided Practice [Demonstrate]*

- Have students practice working in pairs using the slider. Students should sound out the word and then say the word to their partner.

*Independent Practice [Practice]*

Place the materials in your ABC center for students to practice the activity during independent work time. Remind them to illustrate their words to verify that they are able to read the word.

*Check for Understanding [Prove]*

- As the students are working in pairs, check for those who seem unsure or hesitant. Note to keep them for pullout during independent work time.

## Attachment

- Accountability Sheet Handout 23

### Differentiation

| Stage 1 | Stage 2 | Stage 3 |
|---|---|---|
| Students in this stage may have only the initial consonant change on their slider and keep the vowel and ending consonant the same. (e.g., hop, top, mop, pop) | Students in this stage may use the same vowel and have both the beginning and ending consonant change. (e.g., hat, fan, sad, rat) | Students in this stage may use blends and digraphs as they create words. (e.g., shop, chop, flop, drop) |

# Handout 23

## Slide-a-Word

Name: _____     Date: _____

Directions: After you create a word on your slider, write it in the blank and draw an illustration that matches the word you have written.

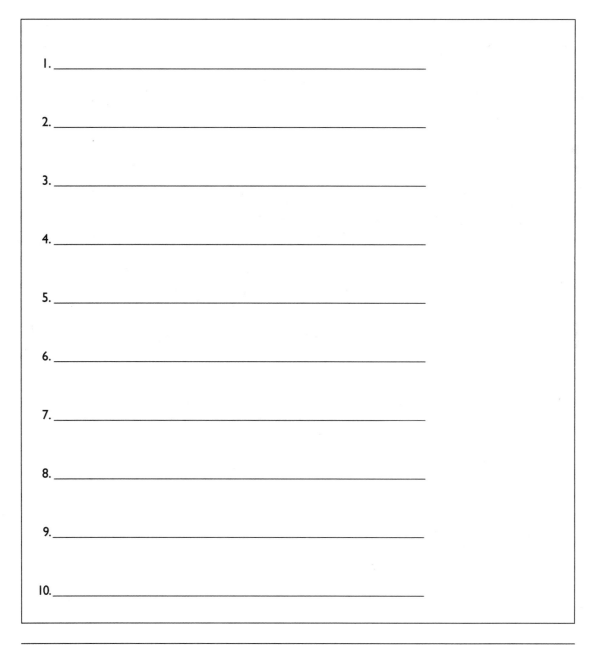

1. _____

2. _____

3. _____

4. _____

5. _____

6. _____

7. _____

8. _____

9. _____

10. _____

## Activity 24: Word Scramble

Purpose: The learner will [TLW] apply knowledge of sounds to build words.

Sample Standard Course of Study [SCOS] Competency Goal Objective:

TLW demonstrate decoding and word recognition strategies and skills (adapted from *Language Arts: First Grade*, n.d.).

### Instructional Strategies

*Input/Modeling [Demonstrate]*

- Explain to students the purpose of the activity (using sounds they know to spell words).
- Show students the overhead transparency accountability sheet that focuses on one phonogram family. Say, ***"All of the words we spell today will have a pattern in them. As we spell these words, I want you to think about what the pattern might be."***
- Show students the first picture. Say, ***"This is a picture of a cat. I see three lines here underneath the word cat, so I know that I will only need three letters to spell cat. But, there's a problem. I have been given six letters to choose from. I need to decide which letters I am going to use to spell cat."***
- ***"Help me say the first sound in cat. /c/ Which of these letters makes the /c/ sound? I'm going to look up at the sound cards on the wall to check. I think it is the letter 'c.' So in the first blank, I will write the letter 'c'."***
- ***"Now for the second sound. I know the first sound is /c/. Stretch the word out /ccccaaaa/. The second sound is /a/. Which of these letters makes the /a/ sound? I'm going to look up at the sound cards on the wall to double check. I think it is the letter 'a', so I will write the letter 'a' in the second blank."***
- ***"Now for the third sound. I know the first sound is /c/, and I know the second sound is /a/. The third sound I hear is /t/. Which letter makes the /t/ sound? I'm going to look up at the sound cards on the***

### Grouping Strategies

| Whole Group | Small Group | Independent |
|---|---|---|
| Materials: | Materials: | Materials: |
| • Transparency of accountability sheet HO24 focusing on one phonogram family. <br> • Highlighter | • Accountability sheet HO24—I per pair <br> • Pencils | • Accountability sheet HO24 <br> • Pencils |

*wall to double check. I think it is the letter 't.' Now I have spelled the word 'cat.'"*

- Repeat with another picture using the same modeling procedure as above.

*Guided Practice [Demonstrate]*

- Have students work together in pairs to complete the rest of the accountability sheet.

*Independent Practice [Practice]*

Place the materials in the ABC center for students to complete during independent work time.

*Check for Understanding [Prove]*

- Note the students who are having difficulty for pullout groups during independent work time.

## Attachments

- Accountability Sheet Handouts 24 (a–d)

### Differentiation

| Stage 1 | Stage 2 | Stage 3 |
| --- | --- | --- |
| Students in this stage should focus on only one phonogram pattern on each page. | Students in this stage should focus on having the same short vowel but different beginning and ending consonant sounds. | Students in this stage should focus on having a variety of CVC words on their accountability sheet.<br><br>Note: Once students have mastered the process, you may use a variety of words and patterns to expand the activity to include four + letter words. |

# Handout 24a

## Word Scramble—Same Phonogram Pattern

Name: _____  Date: _____

n c a d o t

t f e r a v

k t j a b

l o h c t a

# Handout 24b

## Word Scramble—Same Short Vowel

Name: _____    Date: _____

j f e n a t

g c u b s a

p s o t n a

l o b c t a

# Handout 24c

## Word Scramble—CVC patterns

Name: _____  Date: _____

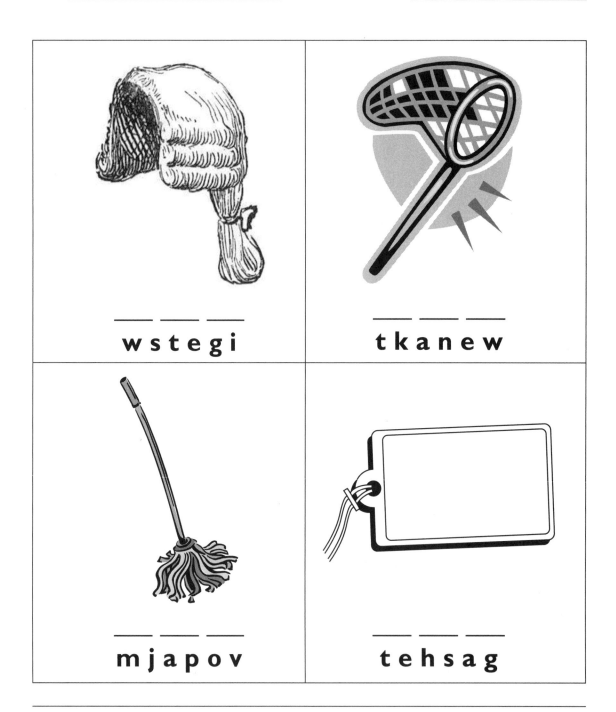

___ ___ ___ ___ ___

**w s t e g i**

___ ___ ___ ___ ___

**t k a n e w**

___ ___ ___ ___ ___

**m j a p o v**

___ ___ ___ ___ ___

**t e h s a g**

# Handout 24d

## Word Scramble

Name: _____          Date: _____

n c a d o t

t f e r a v

k t j a b

l o h c t a

# Activity 25: Word Maker

Purpose: The learner will [TLW] match initial consonants, blends, and diagraphs with word families to make words.

Sample Standard Course of Study [SCOS] Competency Goal Objective:

TLW demonstrate decoding and word recognition strategies and skills (adapted from *Language Arts: First Grade,* n.d.).

## Grouping Strategies

| Whole Group and Small Group | Independent |
|---|---|
| Materials: <br><br> • Large index cards with onsets on half (single consonants) and common short vowel rimes on the others <br><br> *Optional:* <br><br> *Accountability sheets for students to record their work. HO25* | Materials: <br><br> • Large index cards with onsets on half (single consonants) and common short vowel rimes on the others <br> • Crayons <br> • Pencils <br> • Accountability sheet for students to record their work HO25 |

## Instructional Strategies

*Input/Modeling [Demonstrate]*

- Explain to students the purpose of the activity: (making words)
- Choose a student to work with you in front of the class.
- Say: **"I am going to draw five cards from this deck of cards. My partner, _____, will also draw five cards. Now we are going to place our cards face up so we can try to make words with them."**
- **"Now, we will try to put our cards together to make a word."** Show the students how you can use your cards to make a word and have your partner do the same. Once you both have made all the words you can from the cards dealt, say, **"We have made all the words we can with the cards we have, so now we will take turns drawing cards from the pile. Each time a new word is made, you may draw two more cards. If you cannot make a word, you draw only one card."**
- Model both of these examples in front of the class. Show the children that play continues until all the letter cards are used up.

*Guided Practice [Demonstrate]*

- Have the students work in pairs with a set of cards. Play the game through to make sure they understand the directions and concept.

# Letter Cards

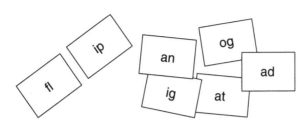

*Independent Practice [Practice]*

Students may work independently with the word maker cards to generate and record as many words as possible. For accountability purposes, students should compile a list of the words they made and record them on their paper. An illustration of each word (if possible) should accompany each recorded word.

*Check for Understanding [Prove]*

- As the students are working, note the students who are having difficulty for pullout groups during independent work time.

## Differentiation

| Stage 1 | Stage 2 | Stage 3 |
|---|---|---|
| Students in this stage should work with initial consonants as the onsets and with short vowel rimes. | Students in this stage should work with blends and digraphs as the onsets and with short vowel rimes. | Students in this stage should use blends and digraphs as the onsets and use rimes such as *ish, ash, ush, ing, ang, ast, ust, ank, ink, ump, amp, ack, ell,* and *all.* |

## Attachments

- Accountability Sheet Handouts 25(a–b)

# Handout 25a

## Word Maker

Name: _____   Date: _____

Directions: After you have created your words with your cards, record your words on the lines provided. Then make five sentences using as many of the words as you can on the back side of this paper.

| | |
|---|---|
| 1. | 2. |
| 3. | 4. |
| 5. | 6. |
| 7. | 8. |
| 9. | 10. |
| 11. | 12. |
| 13. | 14. |
| 15. | 16. |
| 17. | 18. |
| 19. | 20. |
| 21. | 22. |
| 23. | 24. |
| 25. | 26. |
| 27. | 28. |
| 29. | 30. |

# Handout 25b

_____

_____

_____

_____

_____

_____

_____

_____

_____

_____

_____

_____

_____

_____

_____

_____

_____

_____

_____

_____

_____

## Activity 26: Roll the Dice

Purpose: The learner will [TLW] review word families and build automaticity with words.

Sample Standard Course of Study [SCOS] Competency Goal Objective:

TLW demonstrate decoding and word recognition strategies and skills (adapted from *Language Arts: First Grade*, n.d.).

## Grouping Strategies

| Whole Group | Small Group and Independent |
|---|---|
| Materials: | Materials: |
| • Cube with four contrasting word families (e.g., -an, -ap, -at, and -ag). One blank side is labeled Lose a Turn, and the other is labeled Roll Again (see below). <br> • Two markers <br> • Two pieces of chart paper <br> • Accountability sheet HO26 | • Cube with four contrasting word families (e.g., -an, -ap, -at, and -ag). One blank side is labeled Lose a Turn, and the other is labeled Roll Again (see below). <br> • Pencil <br> • Paper <br> • Accountability sheet HO26 |

### Instructional Strategies

*Input/Modeling [Demonstrate]*

- Explain to students the purpose of the activity: (making words).
- Explain to the students that this game can be played with 2–4 players.
- Say: *"Today we will play a new word game. I need a student to help me."* Pick a student to help.
- *"I have a cube here with word families on four sides, Lose a Turn on one side, and Roll Again on one side. I am going to roll the cube and if it lands on a word family, I must say and write a word from that family here on my paper."* Roll the cube and follow the directions or create a word and write the word on your chart.
- *"Here we go! I landed on the _____ word family. I need to make up a word that ends with _____. I know the word _____ so I will record that word on my paper. Let me sound out the first part /___/, and I know I must add this last part from my cube."* Write the word on your paper. Let the student partner roll the cube and record his or her word on the paper as you both think aloud the process.
- *"Now, you must keep your own lists, just as we have shown you. You may use a word only once, so you must pay attention to the words your partner creates. If you cannot think of a word or if you land on Lose a Turn, you pass the cube on to the next player. If you land on Roll Again, you may roll again. The game ends when I call time."*

*Guided Practice [Demonstrate]*

- Have the students practice the game for an allotted amount of time in groups of four while you support their efforts.

*Independent Practice [Practice]*

Place this in a word study center for play during independent work time. Students should give completed papers with the list of recorded words to the teacher for accountability purposes.

*Check for Understanding [Prove]*

- As you rotate around the room, take note of the students who are having difficulty generating words and/or writing the words. Keep them for pull-out groups during independent work time.

## Differentiation

| Stage 1 | Stage 2 | Stage 3 |
|---|---|---|
| Students in this stage may work with simple word families (e.g., -at, -ag, -ed, -in, etc.). | Students in this stage may work with more complex word families (e.g., -and, -ing, -ank, etc.). | Students in this stage may play with words focusing on long vowel patterns (e.g., -ide, -ope, -ate, -ead, -ute, etc.). |

## Attachment

- Accountability Sheet Handout 26

# Handout 26

## Roll the Dice

Name: _____     Date: _____

Directions: Roll the cube. Create a word using the word family you rolled and record the word in the correct column.

| Player 1 | Player 2 | Player 3 | Player 4 |
|----------|----------|----------|----------|
|          |          |          |          |
|          |          |          |          |
|          |          |          |          |
|          |          |          |          |
|          |          |          |          |
|          |          |          |          |
|          |          |          |          |
|          |          |          |          |
|          |          |          |          |
|          |          |          |          |
|          |          |          |          |
|          |          |          |          |

# Activity 27: Match!

Purpose: The learner will [TLW] look for matches of the beginning sounds recently studied in class.

Sample Standard Course of Study [SCOS] Competency Goal Objectives:

TLW demonstrate understanding of the sound of letters (adapted from *Language Arts: Kindergarten*, n.d.).

TLW demonstrate decoding and word recognition strategies and skills (adapted from *Language Arts: First Grade*, n.d.).

## Instructional Strategies

*Input/Modeling [Demonstrate]*

- Explain to students the purpose of the activity: (looking for matches of beginning sounds).
- Say: ***"Today we will be matching beginning sounds in a new game. I need a student to help me."*** Pick a student to help.
- Using the overhead, divide the deck of pictures in half. Keep one half for yourself and give the other half to the student. Explain to the students that you will both turn a picture card face up from your decks at the same time. If the cards begin with the same sound, then the first person to say "Match!" gets to keep the pair.
- If the pictures do not match, continue to turn over sets of cards until a match occurs.
- The leftover cards can be placed back into the pile.

### Grouping Strategies

| Whole Group | Small Group | Independent |
|---|---|---|
| Materials:<br><br>• A set of cards that feature pictures with four to eight different beginning sounds—including at least four pictures for each sound—should be on transparency paper | Materials:<br><br>• A set of cards that feature pictures with four to eight different beginning sounds—one set for each pair of students<br>• Glue<br>• Accountability sheet HO27 or construction paper | Materials:<br><br>• A set of cards that feature pictures with four to eight different beginning sounds<br>• Glue<br>• Accountability sheet HO27 or construction paper |

NOTE: Picture cards from the appendix in *Words Their Way* (Bear, Templeton, & Invernizzi, 1996) work well for this game.

*Guided Practice [Demonstrate]*

- Allow students to practice the game in pairs.

*Independent Practice [Practice]*

Place this game in your ABC center. Each pair of students will need consumable pictures so that they can glue their matches onto construction paper. This accountability allows the teacher to note the matches that were made.

*Check for Understanding [Prove]*

- Note the students who are having difficulty for pullout groups during independent work time.

## Attachments

- Accountability Sheet Handouts 27(a–b)

### Differentiation

| Stage 1 | Stage 2 | Stage 3 |
|---|---|---|
| Students in this stage may play the game with pictures, focusing on matching initial consonant sounds. | Students in this stage may play with words that focus on word families and/or short vowels. | Students in this stage may play with words focusing on long vowel patterns. |

# Handout 27a

## Match!

Name: _____     Date: _____

Directions: Paste your "Matches" in the pairs of boxes below.

| Picture 1 | Picture 2 |
|-----------|-----------|
|           |           |
|           |           |
|           |           |
|           |           |
|           |           |

# Handout 27b

## Match!

| | |
|---|---|
| | |
| | |
| | |
| | |
| | |
| | |

## Activity 28: RINGO!

Purpose: The learner will [TLW] build fluency through word recognition.

Sample Standard Course of Study [SCOS] Competency Goal Objective:

TLW demonstrate decoding and word recognition strategies and skills (adapted from *Language Arts: First Grade*, n.d.).

### Grouping Strategies

#### Whole Group, Small Group, and Independent

Materials:

- RINGO board on transparency HO28 (each box should contain a word from a word family, focusing on two families at a time, e.g., words from the -at and -ag families).
- Cubes or counters

## Instructional Strategies

### Input/Modeling [Demonstrate]

- Explain to students the purpose of the activity: (building word fluency and recognition).
- Say: ***"As I call out a word on the card, I want you to mark it with a counter."***
- Model an example for the children. Explain that RINGO is a game to see who can get four in a row vertically or horizontally (show examples on the card). Also, tell them that they must read the words back to you that they mark and that you will check them.

### Guided Practice [Demonstrate]

- Pass out RINGO cards to each child. Say a word that is on the card. Then have the students cover the square with a counter. Do this until a child calls RINGO! Have that child call out the words back to you (remember four in a row) as you check the answers.

### Independent Practice [Practice]

This game may be placed in the WORD center. Note that this game will need to have a teacher, teacher assistant, or volunteer calling out the list of words. RINGO cards may be changed to reflect the word families being studied.

### Check for Understanding [Prove]

- Note the students who are having difficulty during the word calling as they try to locate the words. Note to pull them out for additional help during independent work time.

**Attachment**

- Handout 28 Blank RINGO Card

## Differentiation

| Stage 1 | Stage 2 | Stage 3 |
|---------|---------|---------|
| Students in this stage need practice locating letters. | Students in this stage may focus on word families that follow a CVC pattern. | Students in this stage may focus on words with blends and digraphs paired with a three letter word family ending (e.g., -ank) |

# Handout 28

## Ringo!

| R | I | N | G | O |
|---|---|---|---|---|
|   |   |   |   |   |
|   |   |   |   |   |
|   |   |   |   |   |
|   |   |   |   |   |
|   |   |   |   |   |

# Activity 29: Go Fish

> Purpose: The learner will [TLW] review word families and build automaticity with words.
>
> Sample Standard Course of Study [SCOS] Competency Goal Objective:
>
> TLW demonstrate decoding and word recognition strategies and skills (adapted from *Language Arts: First Grade*, n.d.).

## Instructional Strategies

*Input/Modeling [Demonstrate]*

- Explain to students the purpose of the activity: (review word families).
- Explain to students that this game can be played with two to four players. Choose a student to work with you at the front of the room.
- Say, ***"First you will mix up the cards in your deck. Then you will deal five cards to each player and leave the rest of the cards in the middle of the table. The object of the game is to make a match with words from the same word family."***
- ***"Now, we will look at our cards to see if we have a word family match. If we do have a match, we can show the cards to each other, and then place our set on the table in a special pile for our matches."*** Place any matches on the table in front of you.
- ***"I have a card in my hand that needs a match, so I want to ask if my partner, _____, has a card that belongs to my card's 'family.' If my partner has a card in my 'family,' then my partner must give it to me and I get to place my match in my pile, and I get another turn."***
- ***"If my partner does not have a match, then my partner will tell me to 'go fish.' Then I pick a card from the middle deck and try to make a match. Then my turn is over."***
- ***"Once my turn is over, the next person asks for a card and we continue to play until someone runs out of cards."***
- Model playing the game until you are sure all students understand how to play the game.

*Guided Practice [Demonstrate]*

- Have students practice in pairs with the game as you observe, clarify, and support.

## Grouping Strategies

| Whole Group and Small Group |
| --- |

Materials:

- Deck of cards with sets of four word family word groups (e.g., that, bat, fat, hat; can, pan, man, fan; stop, hop, mop, pop; etc.)
- Accountability sheet HO29

# Deck of Cards

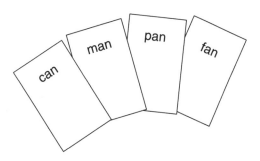

*Independent Practice [Practice]*

Before independent work time, show students the accountability sheet. Explain to them that as they make word matches, they will write the pair of words on their accountability sheet.

*Check for Understanding [Prove]*

- As students are practicing, walk around and take note of students who are having difficulty making pairs/sets. Keep them for pullout during independent work time.

## Attachment

- Accountability Sheet Handout 29

---

### Differentiation

| Stage 1 | Stage 2 | Stage 3 |
|---------|---------|---------|
| Students in this stage might focus only on matching CVC words families. | Students in this stage might focus on using blends and digraphs with the word families being used. | Students in this stage might play the game with more advanced words using blends and digraphs with the various word families. |

# Handout 29

## Go Fish

Name: _____     Date: _____

Directions: When you finish your game, record the pairs of words you matched during the game in the boxes below.

| Word 1 | Word 2 |
|--------|--------|
|        |        |
|        |        |
|        |        |
|        |        |
|        |        |
|        |        |
|        |        |
|        |        |

# 6

## Oral Reading Fluency

*Fluency is important because it provides a bridge between word recognition and comprehension. Because fluent readers do not have to concentrate on decoding the words, they can focus their attention on what the text means. They can make connections among the ideas in the text and between the text and their background knowledge. In other words, fluent readers recognize words and comprehend at the same time. Less fluent readers, however, must focus their attention on figuring out the words, leaving them little attention for understanding the text.*

National Institute for Literacy (2003)

BELS Classroom Activities 30–33 are designed for implementation in sequential order, although the length of time on each strategy depends on the students in your classroom. The lessons were designed so teachers can include other similar selections to teach the same strategy lessons. Also for some of the lessons, suggestions are presented for alternate activities for extension or enrichment. Activities 30a and 30b were designed to teach students how to "read" punctuation the way the author intended. These two lessons should be taught in consecutive order. Activity 31 was designed as a model lesson to teach fluency through phrasing. Activity 32 was designed as a model lesson to teach expressive reading of fonts within a selection, and Activity 33 was designed to teach students to read dialogue with fluency, phrasing, and expression. All of the model lesson may be adapted to many other texts to teach the same concepts as long as your students need the strategy lessons.

# IMPROVING ORAL READING FLUENCY

After reviewing the previous year's oral reading fluency scores for his students, Mr. Foley noticed that almost all of his English-language learners were at some risk of continued problems (e.g., End-of-Year ORF < 40 on DIBELS Benchmark Assessment). He also observed that Nonsense Word Fluency scores reflected that the students had acceptable phonics knowledge and could decode simple three and four letter words sufficiently so he believed their oral reading fluency difficulty was not related to a simple lack of decoding skill. He paired each of the students with a classroom peer who scored above the ORF and NWF benchmarks. During independent work time, the pairs practiced reading punctuation, reading text in phrases rather than single words, and reading dialogue using activities that Mr. Foley prepared for them. They kept track of their progress using simple graphs that they were learning about in math. At the end of each month, Mr. Foley shared their performance improvements with their parents by sending a progress report home. At the end of the year, all of the students were performing at levels comparable to their peers who were not at risk for failure.

## Classroom Activities

Activity 30a: Reading Punctuation

Purpose: The learner will [TLW] read text with fluency: reading punctuation for expression.

Sample Standard Course of Study [SCOS] Competency Goal Objectives:

TLW read aloud independently with fluency and comprehension any text that is appropriately designed for emergent readers.

TLW discuss authors'/speakers' use of different kinds of sentences to interest a reader/listener and communicate a message.

TLW compare authors' use of conventions of language that aid readers including:... punctuation to end a declarative and interrogative sentence (adapted from *Language Arts: First Grade*, n.d.).

TLW read and comprehend both narrative and expository text appropriate for Grade 2.

TLW locate and discuss examples of an author's use of... punctuation (exclamation marks, commas in dates, and to introduce dialogue and quotations).

TLW read aloud with fluency and expression any text appropriate for early independent readers (adapted from *Language Arts: Second Grade*, n.d.).

## Grouping Strategies

| Whole Group and Small Group | Independent |
|---|---|
| Materials: <br><br> • Chart of sentences or TR30a <br> • Highlighter <br> • Punctuation cards (period, exclamation point, question mark) <br> • Masking card for transparency <br><br> *Optional:* <br><br> *HO30a* | Materials: <br><br> • Chart of sentences <br> • Highlighter <br> • Punctuation cards (period, exclamation point, question mark) <br><br> *Optional:* <br><br> *HO30a* |

## Instructional Strategies

*Input/Modeling [Demonstrate]*

- *"Today we are going to practice reading with expression as we notice the punctuation in text."*
- *"We know that when we write a sentence, we must end it with a period, a question mark, or an exclamation point. There are many kinds of punctuation authors use when they write stories. We are going to talk about these three today, and we are going to talk about how to 'read' punctuation. I have a sentence here that I would like to read to show you how reading the punctuation changes our 'tone' of voice."*
- Display Transparency 30a. Show only the first sentence.
- *"I am going to read this sentence to you as it is written, with a period for punctuation."*
- Point to the words as you read the sentence without pausing for breath or changing your tone. *"Wow, that was not very exciting. Now I am going to change the punctuation at the end to an exclamation point and read the same sentence."* Display the next sentence on Transparency 30a.
- *"Did anyone notice anything different when I read it that time?"*
- Monitor/check for understanding. *"Good thinking. Because there was an exclamation point at the end, I read the sentence with lots of excitement."*
- *"Let me try the same sentence again, but this time I will change the punctuation to a question mark."* Show the last sentence on Transparency 30a. Change your voice to make it sound like you are asking a question.
- *"Did anyone notice anything different when I read it that time?"*

- Monitor/check for understanding. *"Good thinking. Because there was a question mark at the end, I read the sentence as if I was asking a question. It also changed the meaning of the sentence. No longer am I excited about my teacher liking me, and I really wasn't sure if she did or not. We call those changes in our voice as we read the punctuation, 'tone.'"*
- Display the punctuation cards for all students to see and point to each one as you discuss the punctuation marks. *"These are the punctuation marks we most often see in our stories. The first one we all know well. It is a period. Whenever we come to a period in a story we know we do not change the tone of our voice. When we see an exclamation mark, we change the tone of our voice to make it sound exciting. When we see a question mark, we change our voice to make it sound like we are asking a real question."*

### Guided Practice [Demonstrate]

- *"This time when I read the sentence, I want you to read it with me. Remember you must change the tone of your voice whenever you see the punctuation mark change."*
- Read the sentences with the students. Change the punctuation marks several times until you are sure the students understand the concept.
- *"Now I am going to give each one of you a copy of the sentences. I want you to practice reading the sentences out loud by yourself to your partner. Your partner is to check to make sure you are reading the punctuation correctly."* You may partner the children for this activity. If you do, make sure you explicitly explain who is to read first. *"As I walk around the room, I want to hear you changing the tone of your voice as you read the punctuation just the way the author intended."*

### Independent Practice [Practice]

Have the students take the sentences/handout home to read expressively to their family. After they have read the sentences, have each person who listened to them sign the handout as evidence that it was read.

### Check for Understanding [Prove]

- Monitor the students as they are reading independently.
- Note the students who are still having difficulty for pullout groups during independent work time.

## Attachment

- Overhead Transparency 30a/black line master Handout 30a

## Differentiation

| Stage 1 | Stage 2 | Stage 3 |
| --- | --- | --- |
| Teach students how to notice ending punctuation (!, ?, .) in stories.<br><br>TR30a | Teach students how to read ending punctuation with different intonations. | Teach students how to read ending punctuation with different intonations and pauses for breath. |

# Transparency/Handout 30a

## Reading Punctuation

I love my teacher and my teacher loves me.

I love my teacher and my teacher loves me!

I love my teacher and my teacher loves me?

## Activity 30b: Reading Punctuation: Period, Exclamation Point, Question Mark

Purpose: The learner will [TLW] read text with fluency: reading punctuation as pauses.

Sample Standard Course of Study [SCOS] Competency Goal Objectives:

TLW read aloud independently with fluency and comprehension any text that is appropriately designed for emergent readers.

TLW discuss authors'/speakers' use of different kinds of sentences to interest a reader/listener and communicate a message.

TLW compare authors' use of conventions of language that aid readers including: . . . punctuation to end a declarative and interrogative sentence (adapted from *Language Arts: First Grade*, n.d.).

TLW read and comprehend both narrative and expository text appropriate for Grade 2.

TLW locate and discuss examples of an author's use of . . . punctuation (exclamation marks, commas in dates, and to introduce dialogue and quotations).

TLW read aloud with fluency and expression any text appropriate for early independent readers (adapted from *Language Arts: Second Grade*, n.d.).

## Instructional Strategies

*Input/Modeling [Demonstrate]*

- ***"Let's do a quick review of identifying the tone of the three punctuation marks we talked about yesterday. I am going to say a sentence aloud. If you think it should end with a period, touch your nose. If you think it should end with an exclamation point, touch your mouth. Finally, if you think it should end with a question mark, touch your head."***

## Grouping Strategies

| Whole Group | Small Group and Independent |
|---|---|
| Materials: | Materials: |
| • Chart stories or TR30b1 and TR30b2 <br> • Punctuation cards (period, exclamation point, question mark) <br> • TR/HO 30b1, TR/HO 30b2 | • Chart stories from transparencies <br> • Punctuation cards (period, exclamation point, question mark) <br> • TR/HO 30b1, TR/HO 30b2 |

- Say the following sentence, changing your expression to match one of the punctuation marks. Check students for understanding by monitoring their signals: "It is going to rain today."—"It is going to rain today!"—"It is going to rain today?"
- *"Super! Today we are going to again practice reading with expression as we notice the punctuation in a complete story, instead of in just one sentence. We know that when we write sentences, we must end them with a period, a question mark, or an exclamation point. I have a story here that I would like to show you. I have typed the story so that it has NO punctuation."*
- Display Transparency 30b1.
- *"I am going to read this story to you as it is written, without punctuation."*
- Point to the words as you read the story without pausing for breath or changing your tone. *"Wow, that was hard! Why do you think I had such a hard time reading that story?"* Accept reasonable answers.
- Monitor/check for understanding. *"Good thinking. Because there is no punctuation, I did not know where to take a breath. Punctuation in a story not only tells us how to change the tone of our voice, it also lets us know when it is a good time to take a breath as we are reading."*
- Display the punctuation cards for all students to see and point to each one as you discuss them. *"Remember, these are the punctuation marks we most often see in our stories. The first one we all know well. It is a period. Whenever we come to a period in a story, we know we can take a breath or pause for a moment, but we do not change the tone of our voice. When we see an exclamation mark, we change the tone of our voice to make it sound exciting; then we take a breath. When we see a question mark, we change our voice to make it sound like we are asking a real question; then we take a breath."* Pause. *"Let me show you just what I mean."*
- Place Transparency 30b2 on the overhead and model for the students how to read the punctuation. *"My, that was much easier and more enjoyable to read."*

*Guided Practice [Demonstrate]*

- *"This time when I read the story, I want you to read it with me. Remember you must change the tone of your voice and take a breath or pause when ever you come to the end of a sentence."*
- Read the story with the students.
- *"Now I am going to give each one of you a copy of the story. I want you to practice reading the story by yourself."* You may partner the children for this activity. If you do, make sure you explicitly explain who is to read what (one page at a time or several paragraphs). *"As I walk around the room, I want to hear you changing the tone of your voice and pausing for a breath as you read the story the way the author intended."*

*Independent Practice [Practice]*

1. Place the story in the reading center for students to continue to practice reading fluently.

2. Have the students take the story/Transparency/Handout 30b1 and Transparency 30b2 home to read expressively to their family. After they have read the story, have each person who listened to them sign the handout as evidence that it was read.

*Check for Understanding [Prove]*

- As the students are signaling, check for correct answers.
- Monitor the students while they read.
- Note the students who are still having difficulty for pullout groups during independent work time.

---

### Differentiation

| Stage 1 | Stage 2 | Stage 3 |
|---------|---------|---------|
| Teach students how to notice ending punctuation (!, ?, .) in stories. | Teach students how to read ending punctuation with different intonations. | Teach students how to read ending punctuation with different intonations and pauses for breath. |

---

## Attachments

- Overhead black line master Transparency/Handout 30b1 and Transparency 30b2.

# Transparency/Handout 30b1

**Reading Punctuation**

My friend and I went to the beach We played in the sand and built a beautiful sand castle We made a tall tower for our princess to live in and we made a moat around our castle to keep out the bad men Then we went to swim in the ocean After we finished swimming we went back to play with our castle When we got back to the beach we could not find our castle anywhere What happened to it We finally realized the ocean had washed our beautiful sand castle away We were disappointed but we decided that we would build a new and better sand castle tomorrow

# Transparency 30b2

**Reading Punctuation**

My friend and I went to the beach. We played in the sand and built a beautiful sand castle. We made a tall tower for our princess to live in and we made a moat around our castle to keep out the bad men. Then we went to swim in the ocean. After we finished swimming we went back to play with our castle. When we got back to the beach, we could not find our castle anywhere! What happened to it? We finally realized the ocean had washed our beautiful sand castle away. We were disappointed but we decided that we would build a new and better sand castle tomorrow!

## Activity 31: Reading Text in Phrases to Promote Fluency

Purpose: The learner will [TLW] read text with fluency: phrasing.

Sample Standard Course of Study [SCOS] Competency Goal Objectives:

TLW read aloud independently with fluency and comprehension any text that is appropriately designed for emergent readers.

TLW discuss authors'/speakers' use of different kinds of sentences to interest a reader/listener and communicate a message.

TLW compare authors' use of conventions of language that aid readers including, . . . punctuation to end a declarative and interrogative sentence (adapted from *Language Arts: First Grade,* n.d.).

TLW read and comprehend both narrative and expository text appropriate for Grade 2.

TLW locate and discuss examples of an author's use of punctuation (exclamation marks, commas in dates, and to introduce dialogue and quotations).

TLW read aloud with fluency and expression any text appropriate for early independent readers (adapted from *Language Arts: Second Grade,* n.d.).

### Grouping Strategies

| Whole Group | Small Group |
|---|---|
| Materials: | Materials: |
| • Chart of "Twinkle, Twinkle Little Star"—mask each word in this poem with sticky notes before you show it to your students. <br> • Typed text of "Twinkle, Twinkle" on overhead transparency, TR31a and TR31b <br> • Student copy of HO31 <br> • Masking card (as needed) <br> • Pointer <br> • Marker | • Chart of "Twinkle, Twinkle Little Star"—mask each word in this poem with sticky notes before you show it to your students. <br> • Student copy of HO31 <br> • Pointer <br> • Marker |
| *Optional:* | *Optional:* |
| *Overhead highlighter sheets* | *Student copy of typed text. TR31a and/or TR31b* |

### Instructional Strategies

*Input/Modeling [Demonstrate]*

- Explain to the students the purpose of today's lesson. ***"We are going to practice another strategy that good readers use. It is called phrasing.***

*What that means is that good readers do not read one word at a time, but they combine words into groups or phrases. Let me show you what I mean."*

- *"First, I am going to say a poem word for word. Then I will read it in phrases."*
- Demonstrate speaking word by word and speaking in phrases as you recite the poem "Twinkle, Twinkle Little Star."
- *"When we speak or read in phrases, it almost feels like we are reading to a musical beat. I am going to say the selection again, and this time I am going to clap/snap/tap after each phrase."*

## Guided Practice [Demonstrate]

- *"Now, I want you to try it with me."*
- Display your chart of "Twinkle, Twinkle" or place Transparency 31a on the overhead and make sure only the title is showing.
- *"Most of you don't even realize that you are reading in phrases. I would like all of you to read this poem with me. The first time we read it I am going to show you only one word at a time."*
- Unmask one word at a time to help students read the poem word by word.
- *"That was pretty hard to do wasn't it? I had a hard time remembering what I had read. That is why reading in phrases is so important. When we read in phrases, it is easier for us to remember what we are reading. It helps us with our comprehension. Now, I want us to read the poem again. Let's see if we can separate the poem into phrases. I want you to clap/snap/tap at the end of each phrase. When you do, I will place a line at the end of that phrase."*
- With your marker, mark the ends of the phrases as the students read the poem.
- *"That was fantastic. See how much easier it was to read the poem this time! Let's read it one more time. Remember, let's clap/snap/tap at the end of each phrase."*
- Place Transparency 31b on the overhead before you begin.

## Check for Understanding [Prove]

- As the children read the poem and clap to the beat, check to see if any students are having difficulty reading the poem in phrases.
- Note the students having difficulty for extra support during independent work time.

## Attachments

- Overhead transparency/black line master Transparency 31a and Transparency 31b
- Activity sheet Handout 31.
- Supplemental selections to teach phrasing

## Differentiation

| Stage 1 | Stage 2 | Stage 3 |
|---------|---------|---------|
| Two word phrases (couplets) only | Two or three word phrases only | Phrases of different lengths interspersed throughout. |

### Other Activities

1. For students who found this task difficult, give them a copy of Handout 31 and work with them to cut the selection into readable phrases. After they are cut apart, have the students line the phrases up from top to bottom. Practice reading the selection by pointing to one phrase at a time and tapping the table at the end of each phrase as they read. You may want them to glue the phrases on a piece of paper for further practice reading at home.

2. For students who need more practice with the lesson above, choose other selections and follow the same procedures until you are confident that they understand the concept of phrasing and are reading with a "rhythm" by clapping, tapping, or snapping after each phrase.

3. You may copy other stories and use a marker to circle the phrases that are to be read. Then practice reading the selection together using those phrases.

4. Finally, encourage students to read selections in phrases without clapping, tapping, or snapping to a beat.

# Transparency 31a

**Phrasing: "Twinkle, Twinkle Little Star"**

**Twinkle, twinkle little star,**

How I wonder what you are.

Up above the world so high,

Like a diamond in the sky.

Twinkle, twinkle little star,

How I wonder what you are.

# Transparency 31b

**Phrasing: "Twinkle, Twinkle Little Star"**

**Twinkle, twinkle/**

**little star,/**

How I wonder/

what you are./

Up above/

the world so high,/

Like a diamond/

in the sky./

Twinkle, twinkle/

little star,/

How I wonder what you are./

# Handout 31

**Phrasing: "Twinkle, Twinkle Little Star"**

**Twinkle, twinkle little star,**

How I wonder what you are.

Up above the world so high,

Like a diamond in the sky.

Twinkle, twinkle little star,

How I wonder what you are.

## Activity 32: Reading Fine and Bold Printed Text as Author Intended

Purpose: The learner will [TLW] read text with fluency: expression.

Sample Standard Course of Study [SCOS] Competency Goal Objectives:

TLW read aloud independently with fluency and comprehension any text that is appropriately designed for emergent readers.

TLW discuss authors'/speakers' use of different kinds of sentences to interest a reader/listener and communicate a message.

TLW compare authors' use of conventions of language that aid readers including: . . . punctuation to end a declarative and interrogative sentence (adapted from *Language Arts: First Grade,* n.d.).

TLW read and comprehend both narrative and expository text appropriate for Grade 2.

TLW locate and discuss examples of an author's use of . . . punctuation (exclamation marks, commas in dates, and to introduce dialogue and quotations).

TLW read aloud with fluency and expression any text appropriate for early independent readers (adapted from *Language Arts: Second Grade,* n.d.).

### Grouping Strategies

| Whole Group | Small Group | Independent |
|---|---|---|
| Materials:<br><br>• Large-print book, such as *Mr. Whisper* by Joy Cowley or other appropriate text, e.g., HO32: "Mary Had a Little Lamb"<br>• Pointer<br><br>*Optional:*<br><br>*Typed text on overhead transparency, e.g., HO32: "Mary Had a Little Lamb"*<br>*Student copy of typed text*<br>*Overhead highlighter sheets* | Materials:<br><br>• Large-print book, such as *Mr. Whisper* by Joy Cowley or other appropriate text (TR/HO32)<br>• Pointer<br><br>*Optional:*<br><br>*Typed text on overhead transparency: TR/HO32*<br>*Student copy of typed text*<br>*Overhead highlighter sheets* | Materials:<br><br>• Large-print book, such as *Mr. Whisper* by Joy Cowley or other appropriate text (TR/HO32)<br><br>*Optional:*<br><br>*Typed text on overhead transparency: TR/HO32*<br>*Student copy of typed text*<br>*Overhead highlighter sheets* |

### Instructional Strategies

*Input/Modeling [Demonstrate]*

- ***"Today we are going to practice reading fluently with expression when we see print that looks different. Let me show you what I mean."***
- Show the students a modified version of the nursery rhyme, "Mary Had a Little Lamb" (Transparency/Handout 32).

- *"This is the story we are going to practice reading with expression. It is titled 'Mary Had a Little Lamb,' and it a famous nursery rhyme. I changed the size of the words to let us know when to read either more loudly or in a whisper. The changing volume when we read this helps to tell the story."*

- Point to the beginning of the story and ask the students, *"Think. How do you think we should read these words? If you think we should read the words loudly, open your mouth wide. If you think we should read the words softly, barely open your mouth. If you think we should read the words normally, touch your nose."*

- Monitor/check for understanding. *"Good thinking. Because the letters are smaller than the ones around them, I want you to read these words more quietly."*

- Place Transparency 32 on the overhead and point to the big, bold words and say, *"Think. How do you think I want us to read these words? Remember, mouth wide = loudly, mouth barely open = quietly, touch nose if it is to be read in a normal voice."* Pause. *"Show me."*

- Monitor/check for understanding. *"Good thinking. Because the letters are larger than the ones around them, we want to read these words louder than the words around them. You all are so smart!"*

- *"Now, I am going to read this story just the way the author intended. I will read some of it in a normal voice, some very quietly, and some loudly."*

- Read the text, modeling expressive reading.

*Guided Practice [Demonstrate]*

- *"This time when I read the story, I want you to read it with me. Remember you must change the volume of your voice whenever you see the size of the print change."*

- Read the story with the students.

- *"Now I am going to give each one of you a copy of the story. I want you to practice reading the story by yourself."* You may partner the children for this activity. If you do, make sure you explicitly explain who is to read what (one page at a time or several paragraphs). *"As I walk around the room, I want to hear you changing the volume of your voice as you read the story the way the author intended."*

*Independent Practice [Practice]*

1. Place the story in the reading center for students to continue to practice reading fluently.

2. Have the students take the story (Handout 32) home to read expressively to their family. After they have read the story, have each person who listened to them sign Handout 32 as evidence that it was read.

*Check for Understanding [Prove]*

- As the students are signaling, check for correct answers.
- Monitor the students as they are reading independently.
- Note the students who are still having difficulty for pullout groups during independent work time.

NOTE: As part of its Sunshine program, the Wright Group (www.Wrightgroup.com) publishes Big Books that are excellent resources for this activity.

## Differentiation

| Stage 1 | Stage 2 | Stage 3 |
|---------|---------|---------|
| Begin by teaching students how to read ending punctuation (!, ?, .) expressively in stories. | Use stories with print that changes size or shape (italicized) as the students are expected to adjust the tone of their voice as they read aloud. | Teach students to read dialogue in a story with fluency, particularly emphasizing phrasing and expression. |

## Attachment

- Overhead Transparency 32/black line master Handout 32

# Transparency/Handout 32

## Reading With Expression: "Mary Had a Little Lamb"

Mary had a little lamb

its fleece was white as snow.

### Everywhere that Mary went

the lamb was sure to go.

It followed her to school one day

## that was against the rules!

It made the children laugh and play

to see a lamb in school.

And so the teacher **threw him out!**

But still he lingered near.

And waited patiently about

'til Mary did appear.

## "What makes the lamb love Mary so?"

the eager children cried.

"Why Mary loves the lamb you know,"

the teacher did reply.

## Activity 33: Reading Dialogue

Purpose: The learner will [TLW] read text with fluency: expression.

Sample Standard Course of Study [SCOS] Competency Goal Objectives:

TLW read aloud independently with fluency and comprehension any text that is appropriately designed for emergent readers.

TLW discuss authors'/speakers' use of different kinds of sentences to interest a reader/listener and communicate a message.

TLW compare authors' use of conventions of language that aid readers including . . . punctuation to end a declarative and interrogative sentence (adapted from *Language Arts: First Grade,* n.d.).

TLW read and comprehend both narrative and expository text appropriate for Grade 2.

TLW locate and discuss examples of an author's use of . . . punctuation (exclamation marks, commas in dates, and to introduce dialogue and quotations).

TLW read aloud with fluency and expression any text appropriate for early independent readers (adapted from *Language Arts: Second Grade,* n.d.).

## Grouping Strategies

| Materials: | Materials: | Materials: |
|---|---|---|
| • Large-print text, such as *The Seed* by Joy Cowley or other appropriate text: TR/HO33 "The Little Seed" <br> • Pointer <br><br> *Optional:* <br><br> *Typed text on overhead transparency:* TR/HO33 "The Little Seed" <br> *Student copy of typed text* <br> *Overhead highlighter sheets* | • Large-print text, such as *The Seed* by Joy Cowley or other appropriate text: TR/HO33 <br> • Pointer <br><br> *Optional:* <br><br> *Typed text on overhead transparency:* TR/HO33 <br> *Student copy of typed text* <br> *Overhead highlighter sheets* | • Large-print text, such as *The Seed* by Joy Cowley or other appropriate text: TR/HO33 <br><br> *Optional:* <br><br> *Typed text on overhead transparency:* TR/HO33 <br> *Student copy of typed text* <br> *Overhead highlighter sheets* |

## Instructional Strategies

*Input/Modeling [Demonstrate]*

- ***"Today we are going to practice reading fluently with expression when we see dialogue, or characters talking, in a story."***

- Show the students the book, the text, or the transparency/handout with the dialogue.
- ***"This is the story we are going to practice reading with expression. It is titled, 'The Little Seed.'"***
- Point to quotation marks on the transparency and explain to the students the purpose of those marks. ***"When authors wants us to know that someone is talking, they use these marks, called quotation marks. Quotation marks indicate when a character is speaking out loud. When I read the words in quotation marks, I like to change my voice to indicate the character's voice in the story. This strategy helps me keep track of who is speaking and helps me understand the story better."***
- ***"There are two characters in this story today. One is a little boy named Juan and one is a little girl named Marcie. I already know in my mind how I can change my voice to sound like I think the characters might sound in the story."***
- Place Transparency 33 on the overhead and read the story. Make sure you change your tone as you speak in the character's voice. ***"Now, I am going to read this story to you. As I read it, I will change my tone only as I come to punctuation that requires me to do so."*** Read the story through to the end.
- ***"What did you notice as I read the story?"***
- Monitor/check for understanding. ***"Good thinking. Because the characters did not speak throughout the book, I changed my voice only when I saw the quotation marks. You all are so smart!"***

---

NOTE: As part of its Sunshine program, the Wright Group (www.Wrightgroup.com) publishes Big Books that are excellent resources for this activity.

### Guided Practice [Demonstrate]

- ***"This time when I read the story, I want you to read it with me. Remember you must change the tone of your voice whenever you see the quotation marks."***
- Read the story with the students.
- ***"Now I am going to give each one of you a copy of the story. I want you to practice reading the story by yourself."*** You may partner the children for this activity. If you do, make sure you explicitly explain who is to read what (one page at a time or several paragraphs). ***"As I walk around the room, I want to hear you changing the tone of your voice as you read the story and the punctuation the way the author intended."***

### Independent Practice [Practice]

1. Place the story in the reading center for students to continue to practice reading fluently.

2. Have the students take the story (Handout 33) home to read expressively to their family. After they have read the story, have each person who listened to them sign the handout as evidence that it was read.

*Check for Understanding [Prove]*

- Monitor the students as they are reading independently.
- Note the students who are still having difficulty for pullout groups during independent work time.

## Differentiation

| Stage 1 | Stage 2 | Stage 3 |
|---------|---------|---------|
| Read aloud a variety of selections to students emphasizing a voice change as different characters speak. | Teach students to read dialogue in a story with fluency, particularly emphasizing phrasing and expression. | Set up a Readers Theater in your classroom and let students practice performing their story in front of an audience. |
| Read stories aloud using different voices for the characters' dialogue. (e.g., *Goldilocks and the Three Bears, The Three Little Pigs, Three Billy Goats Gruff*) | See lesson above for an example. | Have students act out the stories as they play the different characters. |

## Attachment

- Overhead Transparency/black line master Handout 33.

# Transparency/Handout 33

**Reading Dialogue**

## The Little Seed

Juan and Marcie found a seed in the park and planted it near the pond. They checked it every day, but it did not grow.

*"It is not going to grow,"* said Juan.

*"It is never going to grow,"* said Marcie.

It rained for two days and they did not go to the park.

The next day while they were walking near the pond, Juan said,

*"Come and look at this!"*

*"It is a little tree!"*

# References and Resources

Bear, D. R., Templeton, S., & Invernizzi, M. (1996). *Words their way.* New Jersey: Prentice Hall.

Bear, D. R., Invernizzi, M., Templeton, S. & Johnston, F. (2008). *Words their way: Word study for phonics, vocabulary, and spelling instruction* (4th ed.). New Jersey: Pearson/Merrill.

Cunningham, P. M., Hall, D., & Defee, M. (1991). Nonability-grouped, multilevel instruction: A year in a first-grade classroom. *Reading Teacher, 44,* 566–571.

Cunningham, P. M., Hall, D. P., & Defee, M. (1998). Nonability-grouped, multilevel instruction: Eight years later. *Reading Teacher, 51,* 652–664.

Cunningham, P. M., Hall, D. P., & Sigmon, C. (1999). *The teacher's guide to the four blocks.* Greensboro, NC: Carson-Dellosa.

Farstrup, A. E., & Samuels, S. J. (Eds.). (2002). *What research has to say about reading instruction* (3rd ed.). Newark, DE: International Reading Association.

Good, R. H., & Kaminski, R. A. (2002). *Dynamic indicators of basic academic skills: Administration and scoring guide* (6th ed.). Eugene, OR: Institute for the Development of Educational Achievement. Available from University of Oregon Center on Teaching and Learning Web site: http://dibels.uoregon.edu/

Goodman, K. S. (2006). *The truth about DIBELS.* Portsmouth, NH: Heinemann.

International Reading Association. (2001). Supporting young adolescents' literacy learning: A joint position paper of the International Reading Association and National Middle School Association. Retrieved October 26, 2007, from http://www.reading.org/downloads/positions/ps1052_supporting.pdf

International Reading Association. (2007). *Teaching reading well: A synthesis of the International Reading Association's research on teacher preparation for reading instruction.* Newark, DE: Author.

Moats, L. C. (2000). *Speech to print: Language essentials for teachers.* Baltimore, MD: Paul H. Brookes.

National Institute for Literacy. (2003). *Put reading first: The research building blocks of reading instruction* (2nd ed.). Jessup, MD: Author. Available: http://www.nifl.gov/partnershipforreading/publications/PFRbooklet.pdf

National Institute of Child Health and Human Development. (2000a). *Report of the National Reading Panel. Teaching children to read: An evidence-based assessment of the scientific research literature on reading and its implications for reading instruction* (NIH Publication No. 00–4769). Washington, DC: Government Printing Office.

National Institute of Child Health and Human Development. (2000b). *Report of the National Reading Panel. Teaching children to read: An evidence-based assessment of the scientific research literature on reading and its implications for reading instruction* [Online]. Retrieved October 26, 2007, from http://www.nichd.nih.gov/publications/nrp/upload/report.pdf

National Institute of Child Health and Human Development. (2000c). *Report of the National Reading Panel. Teaching children to read: An evidence-based assessment of the scientific research literature on reading and its implications for reading instruction: Reports of the subgroups* (NIH Publication No. 00–4754). Washington, DC: Government Printing Office.

National Reading Panel. (2000). *Teaching children to read: An evidence-based assessment of the scientific research literature on reading and its implications for reading instruction: Reports of the subgroups.* Bethesda, MD: National Institute of Child Health and Human Development. Available: http://www.nationalreadingpanel.org/Publications/subgroups.htm

No Child Left Behind Act of 2001 (NCLB). Retrieved October 26, 2007, from http://www.ed.gov/policy/elsec/leg/esea02/107-110.pdf

Samuels, S. J., & Farstrup, A. E. (Eds.). (2006). *What research has to say about fluency instruction.* Newark, DE: International Reading Association.

Snow, C. E., Burns, M. S., & Griffin, P. (Eds.). (1998). *Preventing reading difficulties in young children.* Washington, DC: National Academy Press.

*Language arts: First grade.* (n.d.). Available from the Public Schools of North Carolina, Standard Course of Study Web site: http://www.ncpublicschools.org/curriculum/languagearts/scos/2004/16grade1

*Language arts: Kindergarten.* (n.d.). Available from the Public Schools of North Carolina, Standard Course of Study Web site: http://www.ncpublicschools.org/curriculum/languagearts/scos/2004/15gradek

*Language arts: Second grade.* (n.d.). Available from the Public Schools of North Carolina, Standard Course of Study Web Site: http://www.ncpublicschools.org/curriculum/languagearts/scos/2004/17grade2

Vaughn, S., & Briggs, K. L. (2003). *Reading in the classroom: Systems for the observation of teaching and learning.* Baltimore, MD: Paul H. Brookes.

# ADDITIONAL READING

Blevins, W. (1998). *Phonics from A to Z.* New York: Scholastic.

Cheyney, W., & Cohen, E. J. (1997). *Focus on phonics: An instructional handbook.* Boca Raton, FL: Florida International University, College of Education.

Cunningham, P. M. (1995). *Phonics they use.* New York: HarperCollins.

Dunn-Rankin, P. (1968). The similarity of lower case letters of the English alphabet. *Journal of Verbal Learning and Verbal Behavior, 7,* 990–995.

Elkonin, D. B. (1963). The psychology of mastery elements of reading. In B. Simon & J. Simon (Eds.), *Educational psychology in the USSR* (pp. 165–179). London: Routledge & Kegan Paul.

Elkonin, D. B. (1973). USSR. In J. Downing (Ed.), *Comparative reading* (pp. 558–580). New York: Macmillan.

English language arts: Standard course of study and grade level competencies: K–12. (n.d.). Retrieved November 11, 2007, from http://www.ncpublicschools.org/docs/curriculum/languagearts/scos/2004/elacurriculumall.pdf

Good, R. H., Simmons, D., Kame'enui, E., Kaminski, R. A., & Wallin, J. (2002). *Summary of decision rules for intensive, strategic, and benchmark instructional recommendations in kindergarten through third grade* (Technical Report No. 11). Eugene: University of Oregon.

Good, R. H., Simmons, D. C., & Kame'enui, E. (2001). The importance and decision making utility of a continuum of fluency-based indicators of foundational reading skills for third-grade high-stakes outcomes. *Scientific Studies of Reading, 5,* 257–288.

Kuhn, M. R., Schwanenflugel, P. J., Morris, R. D., Mandel Morrow, L., Gee Woo, D., Meisinger, E. B., et al. (2006). Teaching children to become fluent and automatic readers. *Journal of Literacy Research, 38,* 357–387.

National Research Council. (1998). *Preventing reading difficulties in young children.* Washington, DC: National Academy Press.

Pinnell, G. S., & Fountas, I. C. (1998). *Word matters.* Portsmouth, NH: Heinemann.

# RESOURCES

## Reading Recovery® Teacher Training Workshop Handouts and Other Materials

A basic guide to ASL: http://www.masterstech-home.com/ASLDict.html

The American Sign Language (ASL) alphabet: http://www.deafblind.com/asl.html

American Sign Language fonts: http://babel.uoregon.edu/yamada/fonts/asl.html

American Sigh Language: http://babel.uoregon.edu/yamada/guides/asl.html

Learning American Sign Language: Using alphabet flash cards: http://www.lessontutor.com/ees_asl_flashcards.html

Teacher Vision: American Sign Language manual alphabet: http://www.teachervision.com/lesson-plans/lesson-2152.html

InfoPlease: American Sign Language and Braille: http://www.infoplease.com/ipa/A0200808.html

SoundKeepers: American Sign Language alphabet: http://www.soundkeepers.com/sign/

ASL alphabet coloring pages: http://www.dltk-teach.com/alphabuddies/asl/

# Index

*Note:* In page references, f indicates figures and t indicates tables.

# Notes

Please feel free to use the following pages to jot down notes on your own stress mastery techniques, tips you've gotten from other teachers, and what works and what doesn't work for your stress level.